To Billy, Scott & Zhema,
This journey started with you and led me home, to me.
Thank you for going first and in the order that my heart could handle.
My love for you is limitless.

To the Woman in the Dark
by Zoe Martin

To the woman in the dark

I hear you cry

I feel your shame

I witness your guilt

I watch you circle around doubting yourself

I see you in the dark

To the woman in the light

I hear your laughter

I feel your heart opening

I witness your courage every day

I watch your love ripple through those around you

I see you in the light

To the woman

I am you

You are me

To the woman

I see you because I am you

And you are me

One

Making Peace With Autism

BY ZOE MARTIN

You are invited into a Mothers heart as she tells you the story of the unbecoming and becoming of her family as one by one, they are diagnosed with Autism.

A letter to my children.

Dear Billy and Zhema

I am writing this letter to you 18th March 2020. This book is going through the final stages then off to be published. I asked you both if I could write about our family story and I promised you both that I would really think about what was ok to share with the world and what wasn't.

You both trusted me and said yes. Billy, you weren't too sure yet agreed in end. You were 8 and 7 at the time.

I don't know how you will feel about this book when you are older. What I do hope is that you will feel and see how much our story is needed out in the Autistic and Neurodivergent community. So many families feel isolated and alone. Parents are disconnected from each other and living and parenting from fear and worry. Homes are filled with yelling, withdrawing, confusion, blame and judgement.

Parents and children are sad and crying and feeling hopeless.

Our family is an example of what is possible when we continue to be curious about ourselves and each other while forgiving and circling back to love as soon as we can.

We are blessed to be alive at a time when humanity is coming together, and we get to be part of bringing acceptance and compassion to this space.

True understanding.

I have told our story (well parts of it) from my heart. I have shared our story so one family may feel more understood. I have shared our story to help families all over the world have a deeper sense of belonging and oneness.

I love you and when the time is right for you and you read this book, I hope you will feel as proud of it as I am.

You have my heart, forever.

Mum & Mama xxx

Copyright © 2020 Zoe Martin
WEB: www.zoemartin.com

First published 2020
Disruptive Publishing
17 Spencer Avenue
Deception Bay QLD 4508
Australia
WEB: www.disruptivepublishing.com.au

Editing Services by Snowflake Productions

Book Cover and Layout Design Copyright ©2020 Maja Creative
Art Direction by Maja Wolnik of Maja Creative
Design by Monika Brzeczek of Maja Creative
WEB: www.majacreative.com

Photography by Greg Dries of Moods Photography

All rights reserved. Without limiting the rights under copyright reserved above, no part of this publication may be reproduced, stored in or introduced in to a database and retrieval system, or transmitted in any form or by any means (electronic, mechanical, photocopying, recording or otherwise) without the prior written permission of both the owner of the copyright and the above publishers.

Although some of the information in this book pertains to matters of health and personal development, it is for information purposes only and it is not intended to replace medical advice in any way, shape or form. If you choose to use any of the information in this book the publisher will assume no responsibility for your actions.

ISBN# 978-0-6486989-6-8 Print
ISBN# 978-0-6486989-7-5 eBook

Contents

FORWARD.. 13
INTRODUCTION... 21
CHAPTER 1... 27
CHAPTER 2... 35
CHAPTER 3... 79
CHAPTER 4.. 111
CHAPTER 5.. 133
CHAPTER 6.. 147
CHAPTER 7.. 167
WHAT NEXT... 175
THANK YOU: 177

Forward...

When I first came into contact with Zoe a number of years ago now, the first thing that I became aware of was her passion and drive to create change.

Not the kind of change that we only lend words to; but real, shouting it from the trenches change.

Podium leadership is dead. People have had enough of the types of leaders who hop up onto the elevated platforms and tell us what to do and how to do it. We've had enough of the people who write the how-to guides and what makes a perfect person or the perfect family..like there is one.

We long for facilitation, collaboration and connection. We feel a kinship with those who bring themselves down from those podiums and sit amongst us.

Human beings need community. In the myriad of ways this looks for a myriad of people as diverse beings, we need community.

We need to know that the person outstretching their hand is the same person who lives the same garden variety, everyday family lives with the same challenges we do.

This is what provides us hope. Knowing that someone else, even just one person, just like us, has found a way to radically accept the beauty within their chaos is what inspires us to move forward. Both on the days where we thrive; and the days we survive.

As a neurodivergent speaker, writer, consultant and parent myself; I know that currently, there are two types of narratives currently on offer inside of any book written by adults raising neurodivergent children.

The first, is the parent who writes about how they overcame autism. They write about the burden of who their children are and how they managed to recover the real child who was trapped somewhere inside.

The second, is the parent who takes on the identity of their neurodivergent children, takes their collective family experience and wraps it up into a story about one member of that family, themselves, forgetting the humanness inside of the family on offer to them.

I know there will be many who will read those last two descriptors and feel confronted. I know I would have once upon a time. As parents to neurodivergent children, we all begin somewhere. And sometimes, that "somewhere" is a hopeless and cold initiation into the fear driven panic around therapies, intervention and a desperation to avoid the family breakdown narrative, heavily perpetuated, often by professionals.

For many of us, when our children are identified as autistic, ADHD, PDA, our future is almost readily mapped out for us, without our input.

The story inside of these following pages is one of serious guts. Humour and humility, trauma and joy. Sometimes, it's bloody confronting. Hard to read. But the challenging nature of this family story isn't around hardships associated with parenting neurodivergent children or neurodivergence itself.

It's around self exploration and self discovery away from the confines, limitations and restrictions of social and cultural constructs geared toward neuro-normative standards. The ones that we, autistic people are often challenged by because we think differently, we feel differently and we need to LIVE differently in order to thrive.

This story tells the truth.

Sometimes it's messy. But those moments of connection are what the reader must give their attention to. What truly matters inside of families.

Not what we should be, but what is.

This is a story of what is.

In just a short, few years, I have had the honour of being on the periphery of my beautiful friend's exploration of self and family life, a friendship between us that weaves in and out of one another's stories.

I've had the pleasure of regular check in sessions over video link together where we laugh and cry, take deep breaths in and then back out.

And here you are, my friend. Creating serious change. Real, shouting it from the trenches change.

Kristy Forbes
Autism & Neurodiversity Support
inTune Pathways

Autistic ADHD PDA
BA (Pol Sci) Grad Dip Ed Grad Dip Psych

YOU NEED TO KNOW THIS BEFORE YOU START TO READ THIS BOOK

Being me has never felt so good. So good. Like fist pump, high fives all around good.

Finally, I am living as me.

Right now it is March 2020. The coronavirus epidemic has reached Australia. Such a perfect time for me to be finishing this book and sending it for publishing. For me, it has been an opportunity to gain even more clarity on what matters to me as a woman, a wife and a mother.

I have an intro, ending, the final edit and kaboom – Making Peace with Autism is ready to fly. It could be 2 years from start to published. WOW. I originally told my publisher it would be all done and on the shelf in 3 months. Little did I know this book was going to lead me to my own diagnosis!

I started this book in June 2018. I smashed it out in around 8 weeks. The words flowed so freely. I cried and cried as the book wrote itself. It was healing. It was cathartic.

I then ran away from it. I bolted actually. I was so scared of judgement. I feared I wasn't doing the right thing by my children. I felt my style of writing was too simple. I couldn't remember everything I wrote yet I felt I jumped around at times all over the place and I couldn't follow it let alone you! I had a draft copy printed and would carry it around with me in the hope I would have the guts to complete it. Nope. Every day I would have some type of internal argument with myself.

The more I got out of my own ego and my own way, I could hear my truth. This book was no longer about me and my story. It was now about you, the mother gifted with an autistic child. The father, gifted with a child with autism.

I ran again. I still had a lot of my own stuff to work through. To clear. To heal. To make peace with.

Not a day has gone by since June 2018 that I haven't told myself to finish it. Here I am, finishing it! (FYI and because I need to tell you, it is Tuesday night, 7:41pm 20th October 2020. I know there are little errors here and there and I am not holding on to this anymore. It is time and the kids and I are going to push send and an author is birthed, me!)

When I wrote this book, I didn't know one very important detail – I didn't know that I was autistic, running ADHD/ADD (Attention Deficit Hyperactivity Disorder/Attention Deficit Disorder) wiring with a PDA (Pathological Demand Avoidance) profile.

Now I have read the book from start to finish through my lens of Autism and my goodness, I am so proud of myself and making it thus far in life. Knowing I am autistic has been one of life's best gifts to me.

You may feel at times I skip from one thing to another. I do. I am surprised that I actually recall a lot of the information from 'back then'. Far out, there were times I didn't know my bum from my face let alone which OT or psychologist we saw for what.

My brain can also jump around so I ask you to be patient and hang in there.

I have written this book as if I was talking to you. You may find the language and sentences simple. They are. I speak from my heart and that is how this book has been written. I only know one way of communicating. I call it heart language.

I call myself autistic and I refer to my children as being autistic and also as having autism. They will make their own decisions as to how they refer to themselves. I use a capital and a lower case A for autism/autistic.

Autism is part of my identity. Finding out I am Autistic has gifted me a greater knowledge of how I operate and allowed me to see and love the parts of me that I have not liked. Autism has given me a road map back home, to me. My neurodiversity is something I am proud of.

Thank you for investing your valuable time in reading my book and to all of you that have cheered me on, kept faith in me when I had lost it and kept asking 'how is that book going?'–you are part of the reason it is in your hands right now. Thank you for helping a dream come true.

Welcome to my story of Making Peace with Autism.

Introduction...

HOW OUR MESS HAS BECOME MY MESS-AGE.

When my family was diagnosed with Autism, I couldn't find any mother out there speaking of her journey in a way that resonated with me. Telling me that she is not only surviving but she found her confidence again, she could hear her intuition again, she could find joy and lots of it, in the everyday. Telling me she felt like her heart had been ripped out of her chest and then she got clarity. A mother telling me I was going to go from chaos & confusion to calm and clarity and repeat this cycle an infinite number of times and that it was ok. So ok. It's how the hero's journey is.

I wanted hope. I needed hope. I was grasping for hope. Just a shimmer of light in the darkness. Not from a professional. From a mother on the ground. I felt alone. I felt my heart closing when things were hard and it was at those times that I knew if my heart could open and expand that I could start to create the life I dreamed of for myself and my family. There were support groups on Facebook, but I found them overwhelming and at times not the vibe I needed. In these groups and platforms, I couldn't feel 'my family' belonged in there.

They say when you meet one person with Autism, you've met one person with Autism. That is because no 2 people with Autism are the same.

This book isn't all about Autism – it is about coming to a place of acceptance through radical love for myself and my family. It is about arriving at a place of not being in argument with your reality. A book to give you hope. From hope, I believe we can achieve anything. If we can picture and feel in our bodies that life can be 'better than this', then we can make it better. I am living proof that a life of acceptance, connection and a full heart is possible. At no point will you hear me say it's easy. At no point will you hear me say it isn't painful. At no point will you hear me say it wasn't worth it.

This book tells the story of a family's return home, to their unique version of happiness, to a love beyond the written language and of a mother that found herself and her life's work in the process.

In these pages, you will find me speaking my truth about the dark, traumatic and painful times, and the times that were so epic I thought my heart was literally going to explode out of my body. All this can happen in a second when you are living and parenting on the spectrum.

It has been a fine line for me while writing this book and talking about anyone other than me, especially with Billy and Zhema, as their stories are theirs to own, and they are so young. There are some parts that I haven't shared. Some parts that are so traumatic that they will be kept within our family and not put out to print. If you are a mother with children on the spectrum, you may know what I am talking about.

I guess I won't know until they are older and read the book and can fully understand it if they feel I have wronged them in any way. My intention is to tell our story in the hope of helping others.

I sat them down and told them I was going to write about our story with the intention to reach out to other families. I wanted to help other parents, and that it will help their kids. I tried to put it as simply as I could for them to understand. I was clear on my intention. I told them how scared, worried and alone I had felt and that I didn't want any other Mother to feel that way.

Scott and Zhema were all for it. Zhema said, 'Mum you are a shining light for our family and now you will be a shining light for others.' That girl is one of my biggest cheerleaders. Billy said straight out 'No'. I was not to include him in the book. This can be a standard first response for Billy. I said that was completely 100% ok (while in the back of my mind I was thinking holy hell – that is going to make writing the book interesting, mate!). After about 3 minutes, he turned around and said, 'Mum, it's ok, you can write about me,' to which I thanked him. I then asked the kids what they would say to mums who were crying a lot like I did in the early days, worried about their wonderful children. Billy said, 'Suck it up. There you go, mum. I just wrote your book. Chapter 1 – Suck it up. Chapter 2 – Suck it up.' The three of us laughed and laughed and laughed. You know, some days, there is 100% truth in what he said… I just wouldn't word it that way!

I won't say sit back, relax, grab a cuppa… I will say, read this book in any moment that you can… that could be at school pick-up when you manage to get there 10 minutes early by some magical miracle, or 15 minutes before you close your eyes at night… however and wherever you can fit it in. May you laugh and maybe cry, I hope you feel a little less isolated in your feelings and life, and at times be filled with 'that so is how I feel!' May you have a chance to reflect on your journey with a gentle heart of compassion and forgiveness and look to the future with hope and smiles.

The past is gone. It is a place for reference, reflection, healing and for data. The time is now. Most importantly, I want to connect you back to your intuition. Back to your inner voice. Back to your own inner wisdom that is unique to you and unique to your child. Hook you back up to your confidence – the confidence that is within you. The confidence that is waiting to ignite again. It is there. It has been there all along. There are plenty of professionals and therapists telling us what to do and what not to do. It is now time to follow your own path… a path sacred to you and your children. The path of the Sacred Spectrum Mother.

Lastly, what is true for me now can change as I change and evolve. I am a student of life and continuously doing the deep work so I can show up and serve at my best. What works for my family and me is a journey that will never end and does change. As our hearts open more and more each day so do our capabilities and possibilities. This book has been written from my heart on how I have perceived and felt our journey.

Chapter 1...

IT STARTED WITH A KISS.

I have a 20-years-plus history with my husband Scott. We have been married for 10 years. Scott generally leaves for work on weekdays before the kids and I are awake. I got to see him on the morning of our 10-year anniversary and he said, 'Geez, Z, what a ride it's been...' I smiled and laughed, and he hugged me extra tight. It was one of those moments when time stands still. I was so proud of us... we had lived another 365 days around the sun... together.

Each day we make a conscious choice to choose each other. Our marriage hasn't been rainbows and lollypops. To be honest, until we got at least 8 months post-diagnosis, it has been either really good or absolute crap. The crap times were often. The good times seemed few and far between. The crap times were painful.

Back then, I spent a lot of my time dwelling over the not so great moments. Pulling them apart and over analysing instead of pulling out the wisdom nuggets, learning the lessons that each of the hard times held and moving forward. My heart literally ached. A lot.

We are a united team. Every day we are working in our relationship. Working on our communication skills, our acceptance of our differences and surrendering to our love. Most of the time we hold conversations and really take in what the other person is saying and hear their opinion on things, rather than shutting down and being deep in defence mode. There is a difference between listening and hearing. Do we like each other every second? – no. Do we love each other every second? – yes. For us, there is a difference. We are committed to our vows and committed to our own happiness as well as the happiness of our family. The commitment has always been there. The happiness has been a work in progress. I often say that I wish relationship skills were taught in high school. Skills like listening, communication, honouring difference and that relationships require joint effort. Just like a garden, if you want it to grow, you have to tend to it.

In 2010 we had the surprise arrival of our son Billy at 29 weeks gestation weighing 1310g. He just couldn't wait to meet his parents! That is the story I was running with. The birth itself went well, and Billy was born naturally and spent the next 8 weeks of his life in hospital. Premmie life can be a tough one with 2 steps forward, 1 step back, 3 steps forward, 4 steps back and many sideways. We were one of the lucky ones and got to take our precious boy home, and now we were a family of 3. My grandfather was dying of cancer at this time and died 2 days before Billy was born. It was an extremely emotional time of both joy and sadness for my family. My brother's son was born a few years earlier at 24 weeks and died of complications when he was 10 days old. Our family has seen the best and worst of pre-term births.

Life was ticking along. We had our son safely home and Scott returned to work and I was loving the time with Billy. He was a happy baby. He would laugh and smile and babble on about life. Billy and I did all the usual things. We did mothers group catch-ups with an amazing group of women that I met in special care. Lots of walking with our dog Dolly, and the essential coffee shop stops. I do love an almond latte. A few months went by, and I was a typical first-time premmie mum. So full of gratitude that I got to bring my baby home, and also filled with worry and stress about germs, feeding and sleeping. Stress about everything and anything, really. I was trying to be all things. Super mum. Super wife. Super daughter. Super friend. I had nothing left in the tank let alone extra energy to have sex with my husband!

I remember the day like yesterday (which is surprising because I don't remember a lot of things!). I was in the study on the laptop and it was the middle of the day. Billy was asleep, and Scott was like, 'How about it?' and I thought, *why don't you just do it– be super cool*. Extra points for doing it with no notice and no planning. At that time, I liked to control everything. I liked everything planned out, mapped out, and was not really into surprises. The middle of the day and in the study? *Surely this will qualify me for wife of the century*. And we did it. Scott went for a shower, and then it hit me – I was mid cycle and I was ovulating, and I was pregnant. I knew it. We went through around 18 months all up to conceive Billy, including 1 miscarriage. I knew my cycle. I went to him and said, 'I'm ovulating, and I bet I'm pregnant.' He laughed and said something like, 'Ahh, Z… you are funny.' And you guessed it. I did the stick test, and bingo. Number 2 was on its way. To say that I had 333 breakdowns before the birth would be an understatement. I already had a baby. How would we cope with another one back to back? How would I be able to look after 2 babies?

Zhema was born at 30 weeks weighing 1922g. 13 months between them. Billy was at the development stage of a 9-month-old. He wasn't crawling, just pulling himself along the floor. Zhema spent 5 weeks in hospital. Scott had to stop work 4 weeks before she was born, and he was Billy's full-time carer as I was hospitalised on bedrest at 27 weeks. I was in and out of the labour ward daily and baked her to 30 weeks. We were all super happy with that achievement. Every minute in my belly was a blessing for Zhema. Her birth went to plan, and she was born naturally. Scott made her birth by about 5 minutes. It was now officially game on. Another premmie to care for and another premmie journey to go on while having a little baby boy that still needed so much. Writing this book gave me an opportunity to reflect back on those times and I am in awe of my abilities as a mother. That is something we don't do enough as Mothers – celebrate our epic abilities.

I am so grateful to the universe for her conception that day as I'm not sure if I would have had the guts to have another baby after the trauma of Billy coming so early and the complications and worry that went along with it. What my brother went through – losing his baby – never left my heart. We were advised to not have any more children as they believed the next baby would come before 24 weeks gestation. I was diagnosed with a short cervix after Zhema was born – once the baby gets to around 1000 grams, I struggle to hold them in. Scott had a vasectomy while Zhema was in hospital. We couldn't take the risk of falling pregnant again. We were now a family of 4. Complete, and so blessed.

I had worked in the banking and finance industry since I was 17. I was a mortgage broker when I had the kids. My career had gone from strength to strength, and it was something I am extremely proud of. Back then, I measured a lot of myself on my career. It was something that always went in an upward direction. I was confident and successful. I was appreciated by my clients and employers. I loved what I did. I knew what I was doing, and I did it well. I was now lost. I didn't know what I was doing. I had no control. I had 2 babies and spent most of the days on my own as I wanted to keep the kids at home and safe. I was scared they would get sick or that I would interrupt their routine. I had them sleeping and eating on a set routine. I was controlling anything and everything I could in an uncontrollable situation. Not a good mix.

When Zhema was 7 months old, I took the kids to the GP for a check-up, and I clearly remember my GP saying it was time for me to go back to work. She was right. Time for adult contact. Time for me to get dressed in something other than tights and a t-shirt. No bagging that at all. I love tights and a top. I knew what she meant. I arranged for the kids to go to day care 2 days a week to start with, and our parents helped, and I juggled Thursdays and Fridays off and worked in between the kids' needs.

Motherhood wasn't what I thought it would be.

At all.

To be honest, I don't even know what I thought it would be. What I do know is that I was in argument with it a lot of the time. I couldn't go to the gym when I wanted to. I was carrying my 'baby weight'. I was tired. I resented my husband during the week as he just got to get up and go to work, and I had to get up, get the kids ready and drop them off and go to work. I knew there were mothers that for whatever reason have to put their children in day-care full time from 6 weeks old and would have given anything to be in my position. Knowing that didn't comfort me at all.

Part of me looks back and feels that I was in a state of PTSD after the 2 premmie births, and part of me feels that most of what I felt was normal. I had huge family support, and still do. I don't even let my mind go to what it would have been like without having my family and friends. For everything I was unhappy for, I was grateful for something else. It was a very confusing and emotional time for me in those early years. I feel we have so much pressure as mothers – go to work – not to go to work – you are selfish – get back into shape – stay home – keep the house clean – get dinner on the table – reply to emails/texts/phone calls/social media – and the guilt and advice is endless. Just for the record, my husband does the majority of the cooking, so I never had the dinner-on-the-table pressure. He is a legend. We are all individuals, and what is great for one mum isn't great for the next. The amount of judgement that is thrown around needs to stop. There are no rules or medals here. What is true for one mum may not be true or right for her tomorrow. Kindness and compassion are what we need to throw around. It is free. Give it a go.

We were in survival mode. We were making it work the best we could. I was very up and down. I loved going to work where I was in control and could go to the toilet when I wanted to. I loved the adult interaction. I also loved being with my kids. It broke my heart to drop them to day-care. I knew I had to. For me. For my mental health. For my physical health. For my spiritual health. For my entire being. They were healthy and happy.

I was hanging on.

When you have a premmie baby, they correct their age, and based on age correction they were hitting their milestones. Eyes and hearing were all good. In the first 2 years, we had lots of appointments for check-ups with eyesight, hearing and other development things. It was full on and it was amazing. It was hard. I loved it and I hated it. It was the full range of emotions. From time to time, I compared my kids to my friends' kids who were the same age yet mine were premmie. I would cry that they couldn't pick up a blueberry with their pincer grip like the other kids. I remember one day Mum saying to me that by the time they were all 18 they would all be able to pick up blueberries, walk, roll, sit and drive. I laugh about it now, and that blueberry moment still stays with me today and brings me back to earth.

Chapter 2...

THE PRE-COLLAPSE OF TEAM MARTIN.

Billy loved life. He was a busy boy with big feelings. He loved his little sister, and when she was little, he would kiss her on the head and look out for her. They would chase each other around the house, Zhema in her walker and Billy on his little 3-wheeler bike. Zhema eventually graduated to her 3-wheeler and it was chaos. A good chaos. You had to watch your heels and toes! They would squeal with excitement. There was so much love and fun between them, and it would also go to the absolute opposite in 2 seconds. Billy would get really mad and suddenly lash out at Zhema. We needed to watch him constantly and on the ball.

The teachers at day care and then in pre-prep would joke that Billy was a policeman. Pulling his peers up for this and that. His intolerances shining through. It was mentioned so much that Billy started saying he wanted to be a policeman when he grew up. There was a little mention in pre-prep that he had some social issues with his policing, but we were told it was nothing to be worried about at that stage. His academic abilities were age appropriate. At the end-of-year concert he wouldn't participate. I remember wondering why he was the only child that didn't get up. I was sad in my heart for him. I was sad for me – why my son? I wanted to see him up there singing and doing all the movements. I just cuddled him on my lap during the performance and told him it was all ok. I could sense he felt something was wrong with him. Looking back, I can see there were a lot of little signs that now add up. I have the opinion that it isn't just one thing when looking at signs of neuro-diversities – it is a lot of little things put together.

It was when he was around the age of 4 that my intuition got really loud about Billy. That little voice in my head became a big voice. His reactions to being disciplined were over the top. If he didn't get the colour cup he wanted, he would go into emotional overload and be absolutely distraught. It was becoming clear that something wasn't adding up, but I couldn't put my finger on it. When he would be playing with our friends' kids, I felt that he didn't share his things very well for his age. His emotions were big. Loud. You could say that most 4-year-old kids display these behaviours at times, but to me, something just wasn't quite 'right'. He would line all his cars up in perfect precision. The line was impeccable, and no one was allowed to touch it. Mum noticed a difference between the way her other grandchildren did collage art at this age and the way Billy did it. He lined all his stickers up in perfect rows while his cousins would place their stickers higgledy-piggledy. Billy had this huge need to be first. First to be handed his food. First to be buckled into his seat. First, first, first.

He had to have more water in his cup than Zhema. The biggest piece of cake. He still wants the biggest piece and to be first, but he is starting to accept when this doesn't happen.

Billy struggled with imperfection in others from an early age. This intolerance was even greater with himself. This is something we continue to work on with him, creating an attitude of learning, and value in mistakes and failure. That a mistake is just that – a miss-take. It is interesting as Zhema struggles with imperfection in herself too, yet has compassion for others and their imperfections. Both kids have made huge progress in these areas, and I am so thankful for the input and influence that our therapists, psychologists, school, friends and family have had on my kids. I am so proud of Scott and I and our vulnerability and courage that we have showed our kids about ourselves. This is where the deep learning, self acceptance and growth for our kids has been. As parents, we continue to go first for our kids.

Zhema was cruising along, so I thought. She was full of love and just adored her big brother. She was absolutely besotted with him. Still is. Billy's big feelings would upset her. At the time I put it down to her being a girl and not liking seeing her brother in a state of anger and distress. All in all, Zhema just played the little sister roll to perfection. She was doing ballet at the age of 3.5 years and was struggling with separating from me. She would cry and cry, and they would take her away. That ballet company had a policy that parents could not watch, so it was all behind closed doors. I didn't think too much of it. She was little. They said she was ok after a while and she loved to get her leotard and ballet slippers on, so we continued. Looking back, no other girl cried at that same intensity when they were led away from their carers.

She hated wearing any shoes apart from her ballet slippers. I tried every type of shoe available. I laugh now at the number of shoes over the years that I have tried on that girl's feet. The number of shoes I have bought and passed on to others with the tags on. I just thought she got my secret hippie gene. She still isn't fussed on wearing shoes. Neither am I. Her feet get really hot and that irritates her. The feeling of shoes irritates her. The first thing she does when she gets into the car is rip her shoes off. Every time we would pull up to our destination, I would have to put her shoes back on. It would drive me nuts and I would tell her when we got in the car, 'Leave your shoes on!' You don't know what you don't know. Starting school was a big deal as she was going to wear shoes all day. She did so well to adjust and keep her hot shoes on. I wonder what toll it took and continues to take on her sensory processing cup for the day. Interesting.

Zhema also didn't like the feeling of a lot of clothes, and still doesn't. Billy has some preference and dislikes to fabrics and clothes too. Zhema has way more. Certain fabrics agitate her, and she can struggle with the length of things. She won't wear a ¾ length sleeve. It annoys her that there is a gap. Sometimes, she won't wear ¾ length tights for the same reason. All tags have to be cut off. I let her pick all her clothes now. She is very particular, and sometimes she will wear something once and then not again.

I now just smile and pass the clothes on to family or friends with love. Billy is great with what he is going to wear on any day. 90% of the time, I lay his clothes out and voilà, he will wear them. Happy days. We do a lot of 'outfit and hair rehearsals' the day before an outing or event (school photos, bookweek parade etc.) for Zhema. It helps her so much and removes most of the anxiety and stress on the day. Everyone wins, especially Zhema!

Zhema was the child that coloured in the tile grout with a texter. She drew on her bedroom walls and on her bed linen (and still does). She puts stickers on things she shouldn't. I just came out the other night after a work phone call and she had put craft glue all over her hands and couldn't see a problem with that. This girl loves slime. She loves anything fluffy. She cuts things up in the night. We accept that is part of her identity. Punishing her for this is not the answer for her. We let the natural law of consequences play out where we can. She has a draw in her room that we call 'The Draw of FUN'. You never know what you are could find in that draw and what the state of that object will be in. Before we open it, we laugh and cringe all at once. The suspension is real!

A lot of our focus was on Billy. I guess you oil the squeaky door first. His angry outbursts were getting worse. He was yelling a lot. If things didn't turn out the way he expected, he would go from zero to one hundred in less than a second. He started to slam doors and kick walls. He would strip his bedding and pull the mattress onto his floor. He would throw things in his room. At this point he had never put a hole in a wall… there was always a level of self-control. I started to see pain in his eyes. A pain I couldn't put my finger on. My heart started to constrict. Scott was rolling out the old school parenting, and so was I the majority of the time. It wasn't working. At all. You only know what you know.

We had discussed giving Billy a smack as he was hurting his sister over and over again. We knew he loved her, and he wasn't malicious by nature, but it was becoming clear that she was his easiest target and the one in close reach when the game or life wasn't turning out like he expected. It was agreed upon that the next incident Scott would smack Billy, and that would be the solution to end it all once and for all.

That's right, isn't it? Don't you just give that kid a good hard smack on the leg or bum and all will be sweet? Problem solved. Did it work? NO. We tried the smack thing another couple of times after discussions on when we thought it would have the biggest impact. I think Billy has had 4 smacks in his life and each time it has had no effect on his behaviour. None. What it did do was leave Scott and I feeling sad that we had used force and didn't get that magical (nonexistent!) outcome. We were left even more confused and lost. This was another indication to me that something was going on inside his mind that was out of the box. The best way I can describe the effect of smacking my kids is that it breaks their spirit. You can feel it. You can see it in their eyes. It crushes their soul. It fragments their heart.

The thing with my kids is that when they act out by being rude and yelling and using tone, throwing things, hitting the wall or – at times – me, they are feeling terrible in their bodies. They are out of tools. They are in sensory overload. Their amygdala is in flight, fight or freeze. Their behaviour is a result of the message their brain is telling their body. They don't want to hurt my feelings or upset me in any way. At all. This has been a hard thing for Scott and me to grasp at times. We are making so much progress in not taking their behaviour personally. I am so proud of us. I see so many parents taking their child's behaviour personally and playing the victim like I did (and still do at times).

Our kids are so full of love for Scott and me. Kids are born wired to love their parents. Such a privilege to receive their love. They hug and kiss and cuddle us. They are sorry for their behaviour now within minutes after they have acted out. The pain and regret for what they have done is like neon lights in their eyes. Heart-breaking. When any force or yelling is used in our house, it breaks their heart and then we have a whole new scenario on our hands. A scenario that leads to a broken little human. A little human who doesn't like themselves. A human who thinks something is wrong with them. At this stage in our lives, I was yelling. A lot. My yelling would scare Zhema and she would cry. She would beg me not to yell at Billy. I would yell and then most of the time cry after. It would have been so hard on my kids when I couldn't regulate myself. Really hard. I take full responsibility for those days and the impact on my children. I now get to rebuild the impact of that trauma and restore trust and safety.

I started to hear another voice about Zhema and how sensitive and wise she was. She would say things well beyond her years. She still does. It blows my mind. She is a gift. She would come up to me and pat my arm and say, 'Take a big breath mum, in through your nose and out through your mouth, let that anger go out through your feet. Find your happy place, mum.' My heart would feel like it was being slashed with a machete as I would look down into her eyes and see the tears running down her face. She was afraid. She was scared. She was looking to me for comfort and security. I was afraid. I was scared too.

Zhema's love for her family is something that inspires my heart every day. Her Team Martin 5 (we have a Cavalier King Charles Spaniel called Huggie who makes up the 5th team member) is the most important thing in her life. I was starting to get out of control. My family was spiralling in a downward direction. My cup was empty most of the time. I was so 'deep in it' that I couldn't see a way out.

Billy graduated from the pre-prep program and off to prep he went while Zhema transitioned into the pre-prep program at her day-care centre without any major issues. The kids are one year behind each other at school. She would cry at drop off a lot, but was generally happy to go and see all her little friends and the educators. To me, prep is where it all unravels to a new level for our kids on the spectrum. Start school, they say… it will be great… sit at a desk or in 1 spot on the floor for most of the day, they say… you will love it… sit still and listen and don't talk out of context, they say… raise your hand before you speak, they say… school is awesome, they say..you will make so many new friends, they say! We tell our kids how great it will be before they start school. Not once did it go through my head to talk to my kids about how school might take a bit of adjusting. That they may think it's going to be like pre-prep and day-care and it isn't. That it may take time for it to fall into place – that's if it does fall into place. No one told me as a mum that it may not turn out to be bliss for my kids and us as a family. No one planted the seed that the classroom is a perfect environment for wiring differences to be picked up.

Billy and Zhema like school. We are part of that club where our kids generally enjoy going to school (until it gets towards end of term and then it can be tricky). That is a credit to the school. Big time. Our kids have a lot to navigate at school. I think the learning side of things is the easiest part for my kids. I see the social side of school is where their autism brings them so much confusion, anxiety and stress. So many faces to read. So many different tones of voices to hear. So many rules to follow (this is a big one for my son & his PDA profile). Social injustices. Sitting still. The list goes on.

Scott and I went to his parent-teacher interview at the end of term 1 in prep with his teacher and the inclusion teacher who looks after kids with needs, and they spoke to us about how Billy was always fidgeting, that he yelled out in class a lot, that he policed his peers and had a high level of social justice. He was overly concerned with what others were doing. We were not too surprised at what was said as we saw all that at home. The kids would watch TV in the strangest positions. Zhema would be literally upside-down and Billy would be hanging over something. Our kids didn't just sit on the lounge and watch the TV. They would sit and move around on skateboards inside, lay down on scooter boards, lay over a fit ball. We would find them in what we thought were bizarre and strange positions that are now 'just how it is in our home'. When we go to the movies, they used to last around 10 minutes in the chair and then sit anywhere but on the chair and now we just go with it. They would hang over the barrier in front of us or sit on the stairs. We learnt early on about spatial awareness and proprioception and that they need to move at times to send their body a signal of where they are. The learning around this for me is ongoing. As we continue to use our toolbox from our OT and other therapies, the kids are feeling so much better in their bodies and can be still for so much longer at times. Hang in there mums and dads if this sounds like your little humans.

The big difference here, and still to this day, is that Billy does not get angry at school. He unpacks at home. Oh, I'm not talking about his school bag. I'm talking about his built up emotions and feelings coming out, the release he unleashes to release the internal pressure he has had building up inside him all day long They both do, and 90% of the time it is on my clock. I find it is pretty common that kids unpack on their mums. I used to hate on Scott for it, as he would say, 'They don't do that when you aren't here.'

We would go to paediatrician appointments and the paed would ask Scott for his opinion and he would say, 'I don't see any of it,' and you could feel the tension between us. You could cut the air with a knife.

Now, he says, 'Zoe deals with majority of that, they unpack on her,' and you can feel his respect for me and vice versa. I now treasure the fact that my kids can feel safe and let out their day with me. Notice I said with me and not at me. They do feel safe with their dad, 100%. Scott and I have come to realise that we both bring different traits to parenting and provide different spaces for our kids and that is something we honour in each other now. We used to fight constantly about our different parenting styles. We still do from time to time yet now it is more constructive and something positive always comes out of it. Let me add in here that yes, I do feel grateful that they unpack on me and not at school – that doesn't mean it doesn't affect me. That depends on where my cup is at. How many tools I have for myself at the time. If I am low, I can easily jump in and have a 43yr old tantrum; if I'm full, I can be the Sherpa and help and lead them to safety.

A lot of people are very surprised when I tell them my kids are Autistic as you can't really 'see' it. If you had a video recording live at home back in those dark years, it would be another story. A video now at home still shows a very different reality than what the public eye sees. Most of their Autistic traits come out at home. Now, I can see it as a privilege that I get to help them with that. The teachers have a big enough job at school keeping

Zhema on task and managing her anxiety. Keeping Billy focused on his own work and actions and not on others is also a big one. Kudos to all the teachers we have had on our journey. I thank and honour you all for how you have supported my children while supporting the other 27 or so kids in the class.

Billy had been having short sessions once a week in prep with the school occupational therapist. We were so very grateful. Life went on, and the voice in my head got louder and the feeling in my gut went deeper.

So began what I call the 'grasping' with 'therapists and things'. Fear was rising in me and I wanted to fix the kids. I didn't know what I was playing with and panic started to make its way into my mind. I started to disconnect from my heart. The kids were seeing a homeopath and naturopath. I was trying to get help with Billy's social and emotional struggles as well as Zhema's emotional struggles and asthma. I had heard great things about Salt Rooms, so we did that for a few months. The kids loved playing in the salt. I still long to go back on my own and just sit back in a chair and relax. I reckon it would be next level meditation in a salt room.

Billy finished prep. His love of numbers was clear. He would add up numbers constantly. He loved designing things and doing experiments. I've lost count of the number of experiments he has done. This can entail him pulling 20 things out of the pantry and mixing them up with things he has collected outside while creating a big mess. All the joys and fun of growing up. His best experiment to date is a rocket ship he has; he mixes vinegar and bi-carb soda, and boy does this rocket launch! His report card showed his academic level was good, yet he was having issues with self-regulation in class – the same issues - calling out, policing, fidgeting and sitting still was something he still found difficult. They had him sitting on a spiky cushion and had a band around the bottom of his chair that he could kick against. The school was certainly doing what they could to help him.

You could say that the kids were happy. Well, I thought they were. They had moments of playing well together, and my heart would skip a beat and my cheeks would hurt from smiling, yet there would always be a part of me that was waiting for the meltdown. The tears. Zhema being hurt. When it was going south, it went south fast and with a bang. I would then react, not respond. It would normally look like Scott or I yelling at Billy, grabbing him and sending him to his room, or sitting him in the front room.

We thought that removing him from everyone was the right thing to do. Make him sit and think about what he had done. Make him pay. He would be screaming, and little did we know then that this was not a teaching moment. It was a moment when he needed us the most. A moment when he needed to know we were there for him unconditionally. That we had his back. He was safe with us. He was acting out because he was in sensory overload. His amygdala was in overdrive. He didn't know how to articulate that. Hell, we didn't even know he was in sensory overload let alone know how to help him. We didn't know his behaviour reflected how he was feeling on the inside. We didn't know he was running Autistic wiring. We thought we were rubbish at parenting. How could we get this so wrong all the time and our kids be the way they were? We kept thinking: discipline more, talk more, punish more.

None of it was coming close to working.

Family life was getting worse.

The kids had lots of great things going on in their lives, too. They were both doing so well at swimming lessons. They started swimming lessons at 3 months old. We wanted their lungs to get all the help they could after the premmie births, and it was a great bonding time for us as parents to get in the water with them and see them laugh and play. They still love the water. There are added benefits of swimming for sensory processing – it puts a level of pressure on the body. The other benefit is the controlled breathing to help relax their parasympathetic nervous system. Swimming is great for our kids.

The shower was a great calming tool for Billy. If he was having a meltdown, we would put him in the shower as soon as we could. He likes the water soooooo hot. So hot that it leaves his skin red. Billy is like his dad in so many ways. They both love a hot shower. They stand in the shower the same way. Like father, like son. Both kids do a certain amount of resisting when it comes time to have a shower and usually love it once they are in there. Zhema sings and sings. Billy enjoys the heat. Showering can be huge for kids on the spectrum. There is so many sensory parts at play – the water, the noise, the temperature, the whole getting undressed and dressed again.

As adults, we can take the ease of having a shower for granted. Think of all the steps that go into showering from start to finish. Interesting. Interesting that there is less resistance if I offer them a bath. So many less sensory parts in a bath. More pressure on their bodies, like being in a pool. I always throw in some Epsom salts, Magnesium flakes or essential oils, and now that they are older, I can light a candle for them.

Billy is really active. We are always playing something with him at home – handball, soccer, basketball, cricket…he loves it all. They both like to ride their bikes and scooter. Billy was sporty from the get-go. Loved balls. Throwing, kicking, rolling. Balls ballsballs. He plays soccer and has played tennis and AFL. Zhema loves to join in with the games at home too. She loves reading books and, to this day, reading books brings her great comfort. She reads every night in her bed. It is a great connection moment for us in bed when I read to her and she reads to me. She loves to sing and dance and does Hip Hop. The girl can dance. Movement is so important for our kids for muscle tone, socialisation, sensory processing and proprioception. Movement is a non negotiable in our home. For all 5 of us!

Our family was surviving – barely. We had fun times together, like going to the beach and our camping holidays. There was always underlying concern that, at any moment, there could be a meltdown and we would all be in a mess and it happened a lot in the years gone by. It pretty much summed up our life at this time. Anything we did, anywhere we went, that thought was always floating around in the back of Scott's and my mind. It was like living under a dark cloud that could open up at any second with a raging storm. There was also just a peak of sunshine. My heart was heavy and closed a lot of the time. I was scared. Underneath my smile, I was scared. I didn't know what was happening with my kids.

I struggled to find the joy in my family day in, day out.

It was now 2016, and time for Zhema to start prep and Billy to go into grade 1. Zhema's separation anxiety was getting worse. The teachers had to physically take her from me most mornings. She would cry and cry. I kept telling myself a lot of kids do this. In reality, a lot of kids don't. When you look at a class of 28 and only 1 is doing it, that isn't a lot. She didn't do it when Scott would drop her off once a month or so. I consoled myself with 'it is just a mum thing'. I would leave the school feeling sick and hoping she would have a good day. They teachers would say that she would settle once I left. Billy continued to see an OT. I had taken them both to see an osteopath and they were still seeing the homeopath and naturopath. I was grasping for anything.

The OT had given me a special brush for Billy and each morning I would brush his body. This was to bring about an awareness of where his body was in the world. I would brush and pray, brush and pray. He would get annoyed at me doing it most of the time. Most of the time, I was in such a rush that the vibration and tone I was bringing to him wasn't ideal. I wasn't creating the time and space so it was no wonder it wasn't pleasing to him.

Our energetic connection to our children is real.

They feel us.

They sense our emotions. In my opinion, this is super heightened for Autistic kids. This has been one of the biggest breakthroughs in my journey – my responsibility for my central nervous system and the impact this has had in my family is profound.

Having children that need extra help put a big strain on my work. I had my own mortgage broking business and had the blessing of support staff, so between all of us we kept my work ticking over. It did mean I would have to work a lot at night when the kids went to bed to play constant catch up. I know a lot of parents don't have the privileges that working for yourself can create. Working for yourself also has added pressures. We also sent Billy to see a chiropractor who specialised in applied kinesiology, and Billy went through a program for retained neonatal reflexes. We had to travel about 45 minutes to get to these weekly appointments. It would take around 4 hours out of my working day by the time I left work and signed him in and out of school.

So now I had him seeing a homeopath, naturopath, osteopath, OT and chiro. I was determined to not leave any stone unturned for my son. I was also operating from fear. When you don't know, you don't know. Zhema was still ticking along in the background. I look back and see all the grasping. So many appointments. So much money. So much stress. I wonder what worked and what didn't, and what didn't work due to the stress it caused from having what I now know was way too much intervention. All so relevant.

We were half way through grade 1 for Billy and his OT recommended we take Billy to a psychologist and made suggestions of Billy being on the Spectrum and showing signs of Autism. In my gut, I knew it. I started to research it, and it became clearer and clearer to me as the months went on. Scott was struggling with taking Billy to a psychologist. I was taking Scott's fears personally and playing the victim.

I took Billy to psychologist number 1, and so began another journey. She was great. Billy and I went a few times and then we went as a family and that was super cool. She got to see all of us and how we interacted as a family. I look back and smile at that session. Billy was jumping and climbing all over the lounge that he and I were on. Zhema crawled in like a baby and was talking like one. Scott sat there so tense you could see the veins protruding from his forehead and his leg was bouncing up and down at a rapid speed. I sat there trying to overcompensate for everyone. I did that a lot back then. Oh, life, I love you. Little did I know that eating surrender sandwiches was going to be a huge part of my inner growth.

Little did I know that one by one, we were ALL going to be diagnosed with Autism.

I spent most of my relationship with Scott overcompensating for how he showed up in life. I took it on as my job to try and prove to people that although he may come across as stand-offish that he was a remarkable human – he just looked a little stern at times. He doesn't talk for the sake of talking. He can look tense. He can be very black and white. It makes for an interesting partnership. Now, I can tell in 1 second within hearing his voice or seeing his face if he is in sensory overload or not. It has been an interesting path on the journey to loving and accepting Scott as he is. That may sound strange considering I married him and we have been together for so long.

I love him with all my heart, yet I wanted him to show up differently. I wanted him to be someone he wasn't. To even write that now brings a level of sadness to my heart. The positive is that I don't want that anymore. I believe in a world where we are all free to be ourselves. It was far easier and quicker for me to get to a place of acceptance with the kids and their Autism than it was for me to get to the same place with Scott and myself. The family psychology session went on and we spent most of it telling Billy to stop doing this and that and were confused at the way Zhema was speaking. The psychologist spent most of the time telling us not to worry about it. This is what she wanted to see. You can see here how I was adverse to how my children showed up. I wanted to change them. I wanted someone to fix them so they were 'normal'. I was also looking at Scott at times and thinking, *Geez, get a grip on yourself!* I was uncomfortable with how they were in this environment.

I was in argument with it all and wanted to change them.

The next session Billy and I went to she made comment about Zhema and Scott. Her delivery of the information was spot on. Being a psychologist, she sensed I was dealing with a lot. It was pretty obvious, really. You could smell it – you could see it – you could feel that I was a mess. She casually said it would be a good idea to get Zhema checked out because of the way she spoke at times. Zhema would talk in a baby voice at times and with accents. It wasn't until it was pointed out that we took notice of just how much she did this. I remember sitting there thinking, *are you for real… what drugs are you… I am here to get my son 'fixed', and now you are telling me to get my daughter 'looked' at'?* At this point, Zhema was in prep and the school had made a few comments about her being a bit vague. Her teacher would do things to try and get her attention back in the class room. She loved unicorns and loved yoga and meditation and still leads our family from the front with acceptance and compassion. Now they were inferring that being in unicorn land during class time was not ideal. In reality, it isn't ideal. I used to joke that she lived in unicorn land. Now it wasn't funny. Just like saying Billy was a policeman – the joke wasn't amusing anymore.

She started physical culture in prep, and she would spend the majority of the class doing what she wanted and not the choreography. I used to sit there and smile with another mother and watch her do her own thing. It was magic in motion. Pure innocence of a child. So precious. There was also part of me that would think 'why is she not doing what the other girls are doing?' This is another example to me of the little things that added up for Zhema.

They were saying something needed investigating in my baby girl. I looked both the psychologist and the support school teacher for inclusive education in the eyes on separate occasions and basically said, 'Yeah, thanks for bringing it up, but I only have the capacity to deal with Billy right now.' Looking back, I was so scared and didn't want to deal with it, so I let her fall through the cracks for nearly a year. Notice how my language was 'deal with it'. I was making it all a problem and a negative. When you deal with something, you see it as a problem and a burden. When you get to help, take action, investigate and come up with solutions and plans – it is a gift.

At this point, Billy was creating an identity as a monster. He didn't like himself. He was confused. He couldn't understand why he kept doing the same acts over and over again. The anger outbursts were scaring him, and they were scaring us. I was not going to stop until my son had the help he was entitled to as a human being. At school he wouldn't do any of it. His home life was going south most of the time. He had very little social life as he couldn't handle one. Now I know he used every bit of self-control he had to conform during the day in the school environment and with his peers. When Billy woke, I didn't know how he would come out of his bedroom. He would either come out fairly ok, or he would come out swinging. If Zhema was awake before him, he would come out of his room and, as soon as he saw her, would yell at her, and she would start crying. Within seconds of him being up, the house would be in chaos. I could never understand why he would do that. Nothing had even happened. No one had spoken a word to him.

Why? Why? Why?

I signed up for course number 'infinity' and this particular one helped me so much in educating myself on helping with the sensory and environment issues and not going for the behavioural issues. We were full on targeting behaviour. We weren't looking at supporting his brain and body. I look back on those days now and wonder how I got through them. Those mornings were hell. I was powerless. I was uneducated. I couldn't control him. I thought I was the problem. I thought he was the problem. It was my useless parenting and he didn't respect me. I had lost my confidence. I couldn't hear my intuition. I couldn't have been further from the truth. That boy needed me to be there for him with an open heart, and also to give him space. We still have difficult mornings, and mostly, I use my tools and help him. I take big breaths, give him space, give me space. I love him in that moment. Is it hard? Yes.

Billy has always been big on me using as little words as possible. That is hard for someone like me who can talk under water and loves to chat. He is so good at cutting me off now, and says, 'No offense, Mum, but stop talking. I get it.' That communication hasn't happened over night. I now smile on the inside and outside and say, 'No worries mate. Got it. And thanks for letting me know like you did, very nicely.' I am proud of how he can verbalise what he is feeling and what he needs most of the time, and I am no longer playing the poor victim mum and I don't take offence to it. Quite the opposite. I highlight that I said *most* of the time – depending on the day or second. I was once told to use hand signals with Billy and it works a treat (when I remember). I just look over at him and say, 'Billy,' and give him a thumbs up or down. Still works well.

Like a lot of the pre-diagnosis goings on – when you don't know, you don't know. Now, 85% of the time he comes out in the morning, he comes to me for a cuddle – or, if he isn't feeling that great, he will go to the lounge and sink his head into it and stay in that position until he feels a bit better on the inside. He can also come out and give me a spray straight up, however those times are lessening as he is getting older and our toolboxes grow.

I am learning that although they have had a good rest, their brain isn't fully awake and on deck as soon as they wake up. Neither is mine.

He had great moments of playing and enjoying life, but he was holding on to the terrible times, and so was I. I was like a spy. Constantly looking for the negative, looking for what was 'wrong'. He was too. Monkey see, monkey do. We were spies in our own lives and couldn't see the forest for the trees. Our family was falling apart. Zhema was crying a lot. So was I. At times, I would yell and scream, and Billy would yell and scream back at me. All 3 of us would end up crying some mornings before school. It was a mess. I was in a hole. My marriage was awful. Rotten. Toxic. Scott and I were arguing a lot. We weren't connecting. I was blaming him for everything. Taking it all out on my easiest and closest target. He was shutting down. We didn't like each other most of the time. Something had to change. We needed help. We would have a break from the kids every now and then, and I would tell him how much I loved him and how I was sorry. It was easy to love and like him when the kids weren't around. Yet, if we did get them looked after, I would have so much anxiety about how they were behaving that I wouldn't fully be present where I was. It was always running around in my head. That anxiety has lessened greatly for me as the years roll by. We rarely take time away from the kids jointly. It's just how it is for us right now.

Team Martin were starting to feel isolated. Having people over was too much. We were so tired and stressed. Our cups ran empty more than then ran full. Filling them back then wasn't a priority like it is now. I hardly knew my bum from my face let alone the absolute necessity to fill cups. Sounds ridiculous yet it was true. Scott can have some crazy start times at his job, like 2am, and can work long days. I was working, managing the kids' appointments and doing 99% of the before hustle and 80% of the after school mayhem. I look back now and smile at what Scott and I achieved as a team. The strength of the human spirit blows my mind. We just did it. Did we do it well? Not really, but we did it. Mum always says to me that I have always done what is required in life. I agree. At times I couldn't see it.

Having play dates and kids over wasn't a thing we did. After around 30 minutes the struggles would begin. Scott and I couldn't enjoy ourselves as we were on edge, waiting for the 'moment' to come. I could count on 1 hand the amount of times we had our friends over in the first 5 years of having our kids. I didn't organise play dates until filled with guilt and jealously. I longed to have our friends over. I would hear of them going to other peoples' places, and I wanted to do that. My kids wanted to have their friends over or go to their friends places. It wasn't an option back then.

Our family operated best either together at home or going to parks and open spaces. If we caught up with people for the odd playdate, they were better off at their place or on common ground, and to this day that is still the case the majority of the time. We are blessed with a group of friends that hold space for my family as we are. You can't buy friends like this. We are lucky to have a village of them. Not a lot, by any means, but the ones we have are keepers.

Now we know being open and taking action on what does and doesn't work for my family was a game changer, we arrange short play dates. They are around 2 – 3 hours. It took a long time for me to be grounded and comfortable in what was best for my children and not worry about what any other parents thought of that. I am now very open and up front about this, and I offer to pick one of their mates up for 2-3 hours and am more than happy to drop them back home. Anything more than this results in sensory overload. Things may change as they grow.

The psychologist talked to me about Scott and our history. I knew from what I had researched and read about Autism/Asperger's that Scott sat somewhere on the spectrum. Scott was pretty closed off at this stage, and I found it hard to talk to him, so I kept most of it to myself. He would get angry and raise his voice, and once again I took it personally, like he was raising his voice at me. He wasn't. He was talking sternly and with fear. He was voicing his opinions. He was worried, and he couldn't fix anything, and he raised his voice. Notice how both Scott and I thought the kids needed 'fixing' as if they were broken. Someone fix these kids of ours, and fix them NOW.

My experience has been that fathers struggle with this journey a lot more than mothers. A lot more. They need a lot more time to come around. Time to get their heads around it all. Time. Lots of time. Men are scientifically wired differently to women. They have a different set of instincts to mothers. Now I can see that, and I'm so damn grateful. So grateful. If I had my time over, I would have told Scott everything right from the start, as it was happening. The universe delivers me lessons in numerous forms. This time it delivered the message to communicate with Scott as things happen, as we missed out on $24,000 of funding for early intervention therapies which we could have utilised. I appreciate the lesson and I have taken the wisdom and left the shame and guilt over this.

Since Scott was diagnosed, and I have a toolbox with his name on it, I pick my timing as to when I speak to him, and he knows everything… everything our kids team of therapists and professionals say and everything that I feel in my heart. I forward him all the emails. He is 100% involved in the decision making and I feel so heard and supported by him. I had created the feeling of being alone on this parenting journey when it came to the kids and Autism. I created that. Not anymore. We were a team, a Godzilla epic team (according to the kids that is the highest level of epicness).

Billy continued through grade 1 with psychology and OT on a weekly basis, and both professionals were leading me towards getting an assessment done.

2017 came around, and Billy went into grade 2 and Zhema into grade 1. The kids were blessed with amazing teachers again. Billy's grade 2 teacher had a lot of experience with kids on the spectrum, as did his grade 1 teacher. They both indicated to me that they felt Billy was on the spectrum. It was time. Now I just had to tell Scott. He was already angry and scared. He didn't want his son labelled as anything other than the greatest son to walk this earth. I remember when Billy was born, and we were talking about what he might be when he grows up, and Scott said, 'He could be the macramé champion of Australia, and to me he will be the greatest son in the world.' The psychologist Billy was seeing at the time also suggested we get IQ testing done. This would give us more insight and another level of information that would be helpful, and it was free for Billy because he went to a Catholic school that qualified for this service. We put his name down straight away. It took over a year to get in, but the information given was of great benefit to how Billy operates. We had Zhema's IQ tested as well. Both kids went really well in their testing. It was such a relief for Scott and I that we didn't have any big learning difficulties to contend with at this stage. The tests highlighted how the most efficient ways for them to learn and process information along with bringing to the surface the difficulties.

I was putting off the conversation with Scott. I was worried about his reaction. I would eat and eat and eat to try and numb the anxiety over talking to him. Eating was a go-to for me when I was stressed. He got home from work this day and I just came out with it. I said it had been suggested that Billy undergo assessment for Autism. I remember using the term 'ASD' and not saying the word Autism or Disorder. I told Scott that it would be in Billy's best interest that we went down this path. This was the first time we both got out of our own way for the sake of our son. What I mean by that is both Scott and I had a vision for our son and his life. This wasn't part of it. This was the first of many times we had to get out of our own way for our kids. We had to put our own programming and how we were raised and how society dictates we all should be to the side. Social conditioning had to go. Scott wasn't happy about it but agreed it was best for Billy.

Next step was off to our paediatrician to speak about getting the assessments. Another cost for an appointment to talk about getting an assessment appointment. This is how it is. He spoke to Scott and me about ADHD. My body instantly went 'No – it is Autism.' Who was I to know? I am just the mum. I am constantly learning about honouring my intuition. My inner wisdom. The older I get, the more I am aware of my intuition, and the more I can hear her. I still face-plant from not honouring her. All part of life. This was another one of those times.

The paediatrician suggested we start on a medication for ADHD. We did. It was horrible. We changed paediatricians. I took Billy to the new paediatrician who I felt at the time was more suited to Autism. I knew it wasn't ADHD. I was grasping. Help us. Anyone. Please.

Scott was really struggling with all of this. I wish there were more support groups for dads and more spaces for dads to speak about their experiences and feelings around Autism and all things about raising children on the spectrum from a father's point of view. Ben Hannant, a famous rugby league player, came out in 2018 and shared some of his journey. It was so great that my husband could hear another man talking about it and breaking down. I will never forget Scott's face and emotion as he watched Ben Hannant. There is now the extraordinary documentary called DAD… a film about Autism and fatherhood. It is happening. I am so grateful. So is Scott.

Zhema was starting to display similar outbursts. I needed help. Who had the magic potion or words or spell that would stop this behaviour? I was on my knees. Crying. A lot. I was in a very dark place. I felt no hope. I was playing the victim. I was playing the rescuer. I was playing the problem. The kids unpacking on my watch was taking its toll. I was on the edge. I wanted more for my kids, for my marriage, for my life. I was binging on food trying to numb the feelings, then dieting and restricting. Anything to take away the pain of it all. When I was actually chewing food, I thought of nothing else but the food. I then committed to doing a fitness model body sculpting competition. I had talked about doing it for 10 years. I love the gym and fitness. I have gone to the gym on and off since I was 17. I had breast implants put in a year before. Now I wanted to compete. I did that as a coping mechanism. To run from it all. I took 20 weeks out of 2016 and into 2017.

I overtrained and depleted my body and put so much focus into that to balance what was happening with the kids. Scott had my back the whole time and supported me in doing the competitions. We all have different coping mechanisms. Some drink alcohol, some eat, some buy clothes and bags, some watch Netflix, some compete. In looking back, it kept me sane – well, to a degree. It was like an escape for me. When I was up at 4am doing my 2 hours of cardio before the kids were fully on deck, I thought of nothing else but my eye being on the prize. Then I would kick into mum mode. The kids were supportive of me, too. I sold everyone on the idea. It is all part of my journey, and I can see now that it got me through one of the most difficult times in my life. It has taken time for my body to recover from it all and I wouldn't do it again. It also has shown me where I was in argument with Autism and what I did to get through at the time.

Forever learning.

We had the assessments done and paid for them ourselves. One was with a new psychologist who specialised in spectrum diagnosis, and the other was with OT number 2 that the kids saw briefly. Every day I am grateful for what we have, and what we have done for our kids and we didn't have to wait. It seemed everywhere I turned there was a cost. A cost financially and emotionally.

Billy was diagnosed with Autism Spectrum Disorder Level 1 High Functioning under the new DSM-5. Formerly known as

Asperger's. We missed out on the $12k of funding by 6 months. I was so angry at myself for this for a long time. If I had told Scott and kept him up to date, Billy would have been diagnosed in time for us to get that funding for access to therapies and resources. It was another thing that kept me awake at night and it was also a catalyst in my marriage and my communications with Scott. I look back and I'm grateful for the lesson, and grateful we had the money to proceed with therapy. I got to do a lot of forgiving of myself.

We were getting somewhere. One step in the right direction. On this journey to diagnosis there are so many steps backwards. It is a fist pump moment to get one going forward. I did many happy dances for my son. After the longest few years of my life, the diagnosis was correct. The medication was right for him – for now. His meltdowns were fewer and some at a lower level. Were they still part of our life? Yes. Did I still think we could fix his Autism? Yes. Did I have the attitude that you could fix Autism? Yes. We were far from out of the hole yet I felt like there was a possibility I could lead my family out. For the first time in what felt like forever, I had hope.

Zhema was going ok, I guess. We sorted the squeaky door first, being Billy. Zhema started gymnastics at the start of 2017 to help with her low muscle tone. At school, she was struggling to sit up at her desk and to sit upright on the mat at floor time. At dinner, she would be flopping forward on the dinner table. The kids walked around some nights while eating their dinner.

The school had her sitting on a spiky seat. It was super hard for her for a long time. Super hard. She would tire easily. When we would go on family walks or scooter rides, Zhema wouldn't last long at all and she would complain and complain. She wasn't having a good time at all. We would try and push her so that she could increase her strength. It wasn't enjoyable for any of us. We would think she was just whinging and being lazy. Far from it. That girl is determined. She is brave and courageous, and she does her best. When you don't know, you don't know.

She was the opposite to Billy in many ways. Gymnastics was great for her strength and confidence. She started pilates and was loving it. She is going from strength to strength. When she gets dressed into her hip-hop gear, you can see her rise inside. She stands taller. She is more confident. Movement can sometimes make her feel physically sick. She goes white. It is a mixture of sensory movement overload and anxiety. She is great at recognising it now, and so I am. She isn't coping out. We are now both skilled at knowing when to call it quits and when to encourage her to push on.

It all gets so much better as the years pass. I kept reading that from 4-9yrs are the hardest for Aspie kids. It is certainly looking that way for our journey so far. Billy just turned 9, and we are really seeing him being able to self-regulate a lot more, and his self awareness is improving greatly. He is showing more compassion freely. It is like he has it in lock down sometimes. He is able to articulate his feelings so much more than a year ago.

Do we still have a long way to go? Depends what you think is important. Depends what expectations you have. Where we are is where we are. We are in an incomparable place now to where we were in 2016.

The night of Billy's diagnosis, Scott and I got into bed and he went straight on to Google. After about 30 minutes, he said to me, 'Z, this sounds like me, doesn't it?' I took a deep breath and said, 'Mmmm, sort of.' I had been researching for what seemed like years, and my heart was telling me that Scott had Autistic wiring. We discussed it more, and he wanted to go for his own assessment. He felt that it would help Billy in knowing that Dad has had good full life. There I was, face to face with a man who was displaying courage in the face of immense fear. A father who was going to face something that many wouldn't consider – all in the name of his son. I was married to this man. What a privilege. Off he went for his assessment, and he was diagnosed with Aspergers/Autism. Bang. It was another moment of relief and elation and fear. I could see Scott over the following weeks and months looking back at his life. He said that some of his earlier years made more sense to him, especially around 17 years old. I started asking him lots of questions. At 47 yrs of age, he had a whole bunch of answers and the same amount of questions that came with his diagnosis.

My marriage was now making so much sense, both logically and emotionally.

How Scott showed up made more sense. He did love me. He just wasn't into all the touchy-feely romantic stuff that I was. He literally didn't have those thoughts. He showed his love for me by doing the washing, the cooking, the yard, emptying the rubbish, bathing the kids. I would work a lot of nights with my mortgage broking job and he really was Mr Mum, and not once did you hear him complain. He still does a lot of those jobs. He is hardest working father I know – both inside and outside the home. I could count on one hand the number of times I have heard him complain of anything to do with his life as a father or husband. He had his Sensory Processing Profile completed by an OT and also has Sensory Processing Disorder.

More knowledge.

So, now I had a son and husband on the spectrum. I was educating myself as much as I could. Mum was our biggest cheerleader, and still is. Her research, cooking, advice, help and babysitting has been nothing short of phenomenal. We simply wouldn't be where we are today without her in our corner. Fact.

It was clear that Scott's and my own self-regulation was proving to be the key in our house. When we were in check, the family was happy. If one of us was out of alignment, the 4 of us would slowly go down. Yelling would creep in. Frustration. The fun factor would decrease. Were we nailing our self-regulation? No. I was about to discover, I held the key to my family's truth.

The more research we did, the more it became apparent that Zhema was presenting as a typical Aspie girl. She was full of love and wisdom, she would withdraw into her own world, she was displaying a lot of signs of anxiety. She would say things well beyond her years. Very philosophical. She would move around constantly. At home and at school. There were numerous signs that pointed towards Autism.

She was struggling. You have this fantasy that the lunch break bell rings, and your daughter runs outside just bursting with excitement about catching up with her little friends. Not the case at all. To think that she was spending her breaks in the sick room made my stomach churn, my throat constrict and my heart close. I could physically feel my heart hurt. I couldn't ignore the voice any longer. Off we went to the paed with the assessments that were required. I attended the appointment with the teacher support at Zhema's school, and the paed handed over the diagnosis of Autism – Level 1. Zhema was put on medication at this point, and another heroic journey began.

I sobbed myself to sleep that night.

I woke up and I was on a high. Nothing could stop me. There was a part of me deep down that was devastated that a diagnosis was handed down for all 3. Devastated. At this point, I didn't know that Autism would be the greatest gift I had received in 41 years. I pushed those feelings down and ran with the high. The medication was having a positive effect for Billy. I had a label, a script for Zhema and Google. The psychologist who did the diagnosis for Billy and Scott made me feel like I could handle anything. She was sent to us from the universe for a limited time before she went on maternity leave, and she changed our world, and I am so grateful for her. She told me that we would all be fine. She told me I was the perfect mother for all three of them and we were doing all the right things. I thought between a label and Google I had this covered.

We would 'fix' it.

Little did I know, I was in line for a massive lesson in needing 4 completely different tool boxes – for Zhema, Billy and Scott, and one collectively. See how I forgot about myself here. Billy and Zhema have different ways of showing me they need help, yet a lot of the underlying struggles and difficulties are the same. I was about to be tested and pushed beyond what I thought was humanly possible.

I had an opportunity to learn how to communicate and be in a marriage with Scott all over again. Little did I know, I was going to have to strip my beliefs of 41 years back to zero and rebuild my family from the ground up. Little did I know, I had to go first for them. Little did I know I was the chosen mother to do this.

Once again, we missed the $12,000 of funding for Zhema by 6 months. My anger around this came up again, but didn't stay for too long. This time it turned into determination pretty quickly for Scott and me to make sure we worked hard and had the money to give them all the therapy that we were advised to give them. To this day, they have not missed out on anything that we have felt would benefit them. They also got a lot of therapy and things when I was grasping that they could have done without. We were doing all we could with what we had. Every. Day.

We put Zhema through the retained neonatal reflexes program and she started psychology. We engaged a girl who is so knowledgeable in the food game to come out and go through our kitchen and educate us on what to put in our mouths and what to throw out. I started baking for the kids. They liked some of it and hated some of it. Nothing new here. I find it comical how it is rare if they both like the same thing. I'm not talking about cupcakes. Don't worry, they both love them. I'm talking about healthier versions. I just made a banana oat slice and it came out of the oven and Billy loved it. Zhema said, 'That tastes disgusting!' The next day, Billy wouldn't touch it and Zhema loved it. Oh, the joys of it all! We made a decision as a family that we were going to make an effort to up-scale our nutrition. We started added little bits of goodness to ramp up our meals that were already working – bone broth was put in our spaghetti bolognese sauce, coconut oil in porridge, collagen powder in omelettes, avocado in their smoothies – little tricks here and there. I felt at this point that the only other thing I could do is pack up my family and move to a farm, and that wasn't an option for us. I was doing what I could in the food department, I felt like I was nailing the therapy department. I still have some guilt around the food thing. I do my best with the skills, tools and time I have on any given day.

We continue the natural therapies support path, and we still have a village that supports us. Psychology at the time was going well with Billy. He enjoyed going to the sessions, and I could see the data sinking in. He wasn't able to implement it when he was in sensory overload, but he could talk about it and make sense of it at times when he was cool and calm. That was a big win to me. Awareness is the first step. Can I implement my Zen strategies when I am in sensory overload? Not all of the time – and I am now 43. He was 7 at the time. I am a big believer in mind training when conditions are calm so that when the storm comes, we can call on that mind training. No point trying to mind train at the peak of the storm. Strategies need to be taught and modelled when we are calm so that we have them ingrained and on board for the tricky times. This is also when we get to trial brushing our kids, sitting them on vibrating cushions, using therapy putty, noise cancelling headphones…you get the picture. At the peak of a melt down is not the time.

We had hooked up with another OT (OT number 3) through the school and she was amazing. Zhema was seeing Billy's psychologist too, but I didn't feel it was the right fit for her, and she had this great bond with their OT. We decided she would stick with OT for now, and we are lucky the OT covered a lot of the self-regulation and social issues in what she did. Billy's psychologist agreed that he had made great progression and he could have a break after in excess of 12 months of sessions. What an achievement! That kid is a champion. Always has been. Always will be.

Finding therapists that your kids connect with is critical. Billy does well with clear, firm boundaries, and has a great sense of humour. Zhema is very sensitive to the tone of a voice, and matching her with therapists and coaches that suit her is something we are lucky to have had a good run with. I feel that just like with people or therapists that enter our lives, some are here for a long time and some a short time. Sometimes we get all we need, and it is time for change. Sometimes it just doesn't quite work. Go with your gut and listen to what your child is saying about their experiences. Sit in on sessions if you want to. It is your child and your money.

The high was coming to an end. A breakdown was on its way. I was worn out. Life wasn't a fairy-tale. The diagnosis, the book and google weren't having the effect I dreamed of. Having a husband, house, 2 kids, a dog and my own business wasn't what I had pictured in fairy land. I was binge eating a lot. Emotional eating a lot. My husband and I were 'friends' and argued a lot. Now I had 2 kids and 1 husband on the spectrum. I was the odd one out. I felt no one thought like I did. No one had my wiring. I went into poor me mode again. I was experiencing shame. Guilt. Inadequacy.

The breakdown came. Medication and therapy was a massive support for my children yet didn't 100% fix it. I wanted it fixed now! I still thought you could 'fix it'. It didn't take Autism away. I spent my life getting the kids to and from appointments, paying bills, trying to not over eat and get some exercise in, meditate for 5 minutes here and there. I felt I was failing at so many things. I didn't know what else to do. I wanted to run away. I wanted to stay. I was a mess. On the surface, I am sure everyone outside my home thought I was going ok. I liken it to the duck swimming every so gracefully on the pond. It appears to be just gliding along effortless while underwater it is paddling like mad.

There was a pivotal moment. I was in such a dark place at this point that I thought the answer was to have a break from my marriage and do it all on my own. All I could do was blame Scott and my marriage for the way I was feeling. I couldn't look within and see how unhappy I was with me. With Zoe. I couldn't see how my past hurts kept showing up. I could only look out and point the finger. Little did I know, all the answers I was searching for were deep inside me. I just needed to reach out, get help and unpack those answers.

I started to think about how it would work with money and the day to day operations if Scott and I split up. Our relationship was terrible. We were stressed and disconnected. We were barely friends. We had the odd good moment here and there but all I was focusing on was the bad times. Where your focus goes, energy flows. That was certainly the case here. Scott was having a shower and I went into him and told him I was basically done. I didn't feel I had a choice and I wanted him to move out, so we could have some space. That didn't go down well. He stood there and said that we took our vows and the day we committed to having children those vows took on a whole new meaning. He said he wasn't moving out. He wasn't going anywhere. If I wanted to go, then he told me to move out. He told me that every day I needed to wake up and fight for our marriage, and that it was garbage right now but it would get better. That tough times don't last, and that tough people do. He said that he would stay and fight to the end. I stood there with tears streaming down my face and I said, 'At what cost – my soul?'

That was the lowest point in our marriage. It was a pain I will never have to relive. I know that in my heart. What I realised is that I felt so unloved in myself and my marriage that I wanted Scott to show me he wanted to be here. I didn't love myself deeply enough to see what was really happening. I couldn't see the pain Scott was in. I was so self-centred in my marriage. It wasn't just me. His love language is so different to mine, and I had been in constant confusion about our relationship for the past 20 years. I have had times of feeling unloved, unappreciated and unheard. He felt confused and unappreciated as he was doing everything he could in his way to show me that he loved me. Our ways of feeling love don't all match and we know that now. I was and am loved, I was and am appreciated, and I was and am heard. We have done so much inner work and work together to get to where we are today. To get to a place where we have an open and honest and supportive marriage. Not a perfect marriage. Our marriage.

The unbecoming of my family was in full swing. Something had to change. There is that saying about insanity – doing the same thing over and over again and expecting different results. It was time for change – in me.

And so began the becoming of my family.

Chapter 3...

THE BECOMING OF OUR FAMILY.

Confucius said, 'There is beauty in everything. Some people just can't see it.' I knew deep down there was beauty in Autism, and I wanted to find the path that made sense to me so that I could see it. Feel it. How could there not be absolute unconditional beauty in my children and their Autistic wiring? What I didn't know at the time was that I needed to be able to see and feel that absolute unconditional beauty in myself first before I could see it in them. I needed to fully accept myself first before I could fully accept them.

I will mention this famous quote again – insanity: doing the same thing over and over again and expecting different results. If we want different results, we have to do something different. Our desire to get out of pain must exceed our desire to stay in it. I was in pain. A deep pain. My family was in a place I never dreamt we would be. The pain was taking over my life and my thoughts. An upgrade of our operating software was required. The software that we had been using until now was not going to get us out of this traumatic mess. Our current programming was on out dated. Trust me on this one. Think of me as that good friend that tries something out for you first, so you don't have to go through the ups and downs and trials and error. Living in the dark is not our purpose here on earth. Spending time in the dark is essential. It is part of life. It is also where the wisdom nuggets lay waiting for you to uncover them.

You can thank me later.

It will require us to take baby steps and a shift in focus. We ee ourselves as the person at the centre of our life – at source. You are in charge of making the decisions that have a direct impact on your life. You are the creator of your life. Seeing ourselves at source and as a creator is the antidote to being a victim. When we are in resignation, we are also playing the victim.

There is a huge difference between acceptance and resignation.

Here we start to take responsibility for our actions and work out what we want to create. It was time to bring this family out of this 'we need fixing' 'something is wrong' 'how do I cure Autism?' 'grasping at everything' 'fear dominating thoughts' mentality. How was I going to do this… I was confused, angry, happy, resentful, grateful, tired, full of life, exhausted. The full range of feels.

I think that sometimes the universe lets us get so down and low in our life that literally the only way is up. That seemed to be a pattern for me during most of my life. That old cliché about always learning lessons the hard way, that was me. It would also take numerous face-plants and getting back up to learn particular lessons. Pema Chodron is a Buddhist Nun that I love, respect and admire. Her books are life changing. One of my favourite quotes of hers (I have many) is, 'Only to the extent that we expose ourselves over and over to annihilation can that which is indestructible be found in us.' I can vouch for that. I also now know first-hand that the magic is in getting back up. Life has shown me that on the back of a breakdown is a breakthrough. Every step is a step, and each step takes courage no matter what the result. I continue learning and nothing is a failure. It is only failing if I fail to learn the lesson and take what is meant for me. Life is filled with data. I have no regrets. I have pieces of data that make up my extraordinary life.

After the elation and adrenaline of the diagnosis of my children and husband had left my body, I felt like the last 7 years had caught up with me at once. I felt so much shame around my parenting. Trying to discipline my children for things that I now know were beyond their control. The times I had screamed at Billy and frightened little Zhema. The times I had squeezed Billy's shoulders or given him a smack. Punishing them for acting out. They were in sensory overload and needed my support. Sending them to their bedroom as time out and isolating them gives them a feeling they are alone and unloved. A feeling that they aren't worthy of being around me, and that something is wrong with them. A feeling that they are not worthy of my love. I was blaming myself for their premature births and not being able to physically carry them to full term. Blaming myself for putting them in day-care and not being a stay-at-home mum. Blame. Guilt.

I also hated myself for not following my intuition. For ignoring the voice. For ignoring the 100% fact that nobody knows my children like I do. Nobody. Ignoring the signs. More guilt. More shame. More regret. Do I still have times of doubt and not being enough for them? Yes. I am human, after all. This was a period in my life where I felt I had no 'time'. Most of my waking hours was spent in worry, resentment, anger, comparison, jealousy. I felt like I had no time because my head was full. Full to the brim. No space. Full of thoughts racing around. Grasping. Fearing the worst.

Blame. Shame. Blame. Shame. Shame and guilt are the lowest vibrating emotions that we can experience. They were my predominate state at this stage of my journey. They are also the turning point and portals where you get to see your divinity and step into it. In this darkness and shame came the rise of a woman that I am proud to call me. Now, I let these feelings and thoughts pass through me. Not easy at times, yet always worth it. I breathe and remind myself, 'I am the perfect mother for my children.' I am…

The kids were in therapy. We were doing all the right things by the book. Well, I thought we were. I thought between therapy, the wonderful things the school was doing for them along with Scott and me loving them that it would be enough. Wrong. Our progress had stalled. Overall, home life was still rotten. Scott and I were rotten a lot of the time. I was rotten a lot of the time. I wanted more for our life and it was going to have to be me that went first.

I realised I now had the opportunity to take responsibility for myself and the role I was playing. Me. Yep, mum. I had the opportunity to live with integrity and alignment to my own values and morals. I had the opportunity to lift my self-care game. It was an opportunity to forgive myself. An opportunity to go back over my life and heal my past wounds. I had the opportunity to go deep within and find out how I can get to a place of acceptance and to live with radical love. Acceptance that all my family had been diagnosed with Autism. Life was gifting me an opportunity for me to step into the woman and mother I had longed to be. The woman I knew I could be. The woman I was worthy of being. A woman living a life she was so worthy of living. An opportunity.

Here it was.

I felt like it was lit up in neon lights flashing before me everywhere I went: 'YOUR TIME IS NOW. EMBRACE THIS WITH ALL YOU'VE GOT, OR LIVE WITH A CLOSED

HEART AND IN ARGUMENT WITH LIFE.' I made the choice. I was going to master keeping my heart open and I was going to master what I needed and what my family needed. Mastery to me never ends. Mastery is a daily choice. It is a moment-by-moment choice. Every breath we take is an opportunity to return to love.

I need to make it clear that is it the accumulation of many areas collectively that has pulled me out of the dark hole I lived in. It isn't just one thing. I liken it to juggling balls of self-care, integrity, acceptance, responsibility, alignment, connection, all in the air. All balls need attention and when one falls you are at risk of dropping the others too. If I put too much focus on one ball, then the other balls can crash to the ground. I am learning to be a master at juggling and seeing when the balls are out of sync. To me, the definition of a master is someone that fails continuously yet continues on the path of mastery regardless of failing.

Scott has always said that I set the tone for the house. If I was happy, the household was happy. If I was flustered, the household was flustered. I agree with that – history had certainly proved it time and time again. I used to feel resentful that to a degree I was responsible for everyone and how they felt. That felt super heavy to me. At times, it felt like I was suffocating under the pressure, and that everyone's behaviour was a direct reflection of me. What I now know is that I am responsible for my actions, and my actions have a direct impact on those around me. When kids are struggling and acting out, generally as parents we feel like it is our fault. We are genetically wired to feel we haven't done enough. We haven't done the right things. When they are kicking goals and ticking all the boxes, we feel awesome and stand tall and take credit for that to a certain degree. Conditional.

My family deeply feels my energy. Deeply. It is fact. It is a privilege that I get to honour my energy and the impact it has on them and the collective. My central nervous system is my responsibility and all my family plugs into it. Fact. Imagine there is an energy cord running from your children and partner into you. That cord carries your vibration and feelings back to them.

Let that sink in.

Most days during the pre-diagnosis years and a few months post-diagnosis, I would walk in the door from school pick-up with both kids in toe and be cranky. I was like, 'why do within minutes of getting in the car they start fighting? Why can't we just have one drive home in peace? Why? Why? Why?' I was in complete argument with the way life was. I was lacking acceptance. This is a clear example of feeling like the victim and focusing on the negative and feeling sorry for myself. Seeing the kids as a problem. I had a limited ability to look beyond my own emotions to see what may be affecting the kids. I was listening to David Emerald (he came up with The Power of TED) and he said, 'Fish can't see water.' He was referring to our inability to see all the drama playing out when we are in the middle of it. I was starting to see how my mood rubbed off on the rest of the house and how I would let their moods rub off on me. Big time. This revelation was going to gift me radical self responsibility. An opportunity to take back my identity and gift my family back theirs.

I was going to build a new foundation for this family by going first. Leaders go first. I was going to lead. I was going to take responsibility for my own actions. I was fed up living the way I was and I wanted to live with integrity and ramp up my own bullshit odometer. Time to focus on my behaviour and go within. Within… where all the answers lie. Stop pointing the finger at Autism, at Scott and at the kids. My heart was telling me to point the finger at me. I had 3 humans counting on me. I was counting on me. Self-regulation and self-care was at the forefront of my intuition. It was something I had numbed and made excuses for since as long as I can remember. I yell because of the kid's behaviour. I lost my cool because I was tired. I used tone towards Scott and Mum because something was bothering me about work or I wasn't happy with my weight. Short-fused from eating a block of chocolate. Frustrated during homework time because I hadn't gone for a walk or moved my body that day and I was filled with regret. Notice here how I am completely out of integrity and alignment with myself and my morals. I was avoiding taking responsibility for my self-care and what is important to my minute to minute functioning. Acting out and spewing out blame as I was unhappy with me. It had nothing to do with anyone else but me.

Sobering realisation.

Humans that are autistic can be sensitive to how we are feeling. They have this amazing ability to pick up on our emotions and vibrations. My kids can sense my emotions at times before I can. When I'm deep in victimhood, self-pity or frustration. I used to be the last to see it. Fast forward and they now say to me, 'Mum, you seem overwhelmed.' 'Mum, you are using tone.' 'Mama, you seem flustered.' 'Mama, take a deep breath.' 'Mum, you are being rude.' I have gifted them this language from speaking openly about how I am feeling.

How are kids supposed to be able to label and speak about how they feel if they lack the language for it?

What happens when they can't express themselves in a way that we can understand? Outbursts. Something gets thrown. Someone gets hurt. They withdraw. Shutdown. Meltdown. There were many moments where I have set them off from my own lack of regulation and it hasn't ended well. I own that and turn it into a teaching and learning moment for myself. Other times, they can tell me 'Mum, you are being rude right now and I don't like it. You don't like it when I am rude to you, so don't be rude to me.' In these moments I am so proud of them, and me. Progress.

They are legends at keeping me in my alignment and calling me out on my own stuff. Especially Billy. He loves to hang me out to dry! I have sat down with them countless times and had conversations around the kind of person and mother I want to be, so we are all clear on what I am working on and what my end game is. My end game is to live in a world where we feel free to be ourselves. You can count on me to hold space with an open heart. I stand for radical love and acceptance. I am changing and growing all the time. These conversations will always be the normal in my home. Same goes with Scott. I have conversations around this with him too. It can be super uncomfortable. Conversations where I have had to dig deep into my heart and pull out all of my courage. These times can get you smack bang in your guts. Some of my greatest connections to the ones I love are the outcome of these vulnerable conversations. To put my ego aside and show up bearing all takes courage and guts, and it is something I have never regretted doing. Ever.

I sit before my husband and kids and say, 'I love you every minute of every day and I'm sorry for…'. Everyone then knows I am aware that I am out of my alignment and that I am committed to being the best version of myself. The kids can then turn around and tell me in their words what they are working on within themselves. After they yell at me, they will come to me and say things like, 'Mum, I am sorry I yelled. That isn't the daughter/son I want to be and I'm working hard to stop yelling. I was angry that such-and-such happened'. That opens up the conversation around what happened, and we can chat about solutions and strategies we can use next time. This is the point that it turns into a teaching moment. Forgiveness and acceptance rises.

When looking at my self-regulation, I had to work out what was setting me off. What were my triggers? Why did all the little things add up to big things, or why did a little thing set me off? We all have a pressure release valve. What were my pressures? Where did I want them in my life and where didn't I? How was I releasing the pressure? One thing I say often is, 'I never thought in my wildest dreams that Autism would be one of the greatest gifts I have ever received.' And what I mean by that is that without the diagnosis and realisation that the way I walked around and lived life would have a 100% direct impact on my children's mental and physical health, I could still well be living this life in victim mode a lot of the time.

As I said before, leaders go first. As their mother, you get to go first. You get to lead. You get to demonstrate taking big deep breaths when you feel like exploding. You get to demonstrate what going slow and enjoying your version of your life looks like. You get to demonstrate that anger is part of being human and there are ways to channel it. You get to demonstrate social skills and show them kindness and compassion both for yourself and others and that we all come in different shapes, sizes and personalities. You. It was *you* they trusted to house them for 9 months (give or take). It is *you* that has the wisdom and intuition to help guide, coach, support and mentor them along the way.

Trust that you are enough. Always.

One of my triggers was my resignation about my family's 'different' wiring system. Resignation is like, 'oh well. This is how it is.' As Billy said – suck it up. Cop it on the chin, mate. These are the cards you have been dealt, so just get over it. When you live in resignation, you will spend your days being pulled in 2 different directions and living in argument with the way things are. This is because your heart and soul are trying to show you the power in yourself and the beauty in your situation, but you feel powerless and a failure and it's all too hard, so you just throw all your toys out of your cot and say, 'This is just how it is – suck it up, princess!' You feel hopeless. Resignation breeds resentment. If you are reading this book then I'm pretty certain that there is a little voice in you that you can hear if you allow yourself to and it is telling you, 'Come on, things can be better than this, you know they can be better than this.' That voice is right!

Acceptance, to me, is being able to embrace the diversity of my family. To be able to sit back in those quiet moments when everyone is in bed and feel in my heart that this is exactly where I am meant to be. Being able to say the word Autism and not feel sick or shame or my throat tighten. Saying the word 'Autism' and feeling my chest rise with pride and a gentle smile opening on my face. Keeping your heart open when your child is hitting you, calling you names, hurting their sibling or another child, yelling at their mates, not wanting to leave the house due to anxiety, constantly complaining they feel sick like a big ball of fat is slamming around in their belly – that is acceptance.

Acceptance is meeting every sentient being exactly where they are at.

When I can change plans 3 times because what I originally thought was going to work for us doesn't. When I can leave the movie theatre a quarter of the way through a movie because it just isn't our day. When I text a mum and say I am dropping their child back home after half an hour as it isn't working out. When I sit on the end of their bed after being hit and yelled at and told to get out and be ready to give them a cuddle the moment they ask for it. When I speak our truth and let friends know that these times or places work for us. Looking my kids in the eye when they cry and ask if something is wrong with them and I tell them, 'No, there is nothing wrong with you, you are human and there is no one as epic as you.' When people come over and ask why we have a mini trampoline in the middle of our lounge room and I don't even think twice and say, 'Oh that is what works here – have a go – jump on it then jump on the lounge – it is fun.' When it is best for my kids to do some of their homework while spinning on a chair or playing handball. When it is best that Scott and I do all the writing that is required sometimes with homework. When I can hold them tight while they are crying, and I am crying and tell them I don't know what to do right now but what I do know is that I love you every minute of every day and every night and nothing they can do will ever change that. Ever.

When I can do these things from an open heart and a place of love – this is acceptance, and they feel it.

Where am I at with acceptance? Great question. At times I still collapse acceptance and resignation together. I think I am living in acceptance and walking around like, 'This is all part of life with Autism, just take a deep breath and go again,' yet I can feel in my body it is resignation and the little voice is saying, 'Again? Really?' Acceptance for me in this situation sounds to me like, 'What is required of me right now?' 'What can I do to support my children's brains and bodies right now?' 'What is my heart trying to tell me?' 'What is their heart trying to tell me?'.

I am living way more in acceptance than resignation these days, and when I do cross over into resignation, it isn't for long. I am human. 100%. So are you. I can catch myself there and go, 'Ok Zoe, what do YOU need right now?' or 'Hello judgement my old friend, what really brings you here right now?' It could be as simple of having a cup of herbal tea, putting on a cool song and having a boogie, scheduling time on my own, getting the kids and dog and going for a walk or scooter, kissing the kids and hugging them and asking them for a big squeezy hug back; it could be reminding myself that I am human, that I am the chosen mother for them, or taking a big breath. Breathing is my super power! It could mean going into the study, pulling out a notepad and brain dumping all the open tabs I have in my mind. Getting the 'to do list' down on paper and out of my mind. It could mean carving out time to close those open tabs and ring and make the appointments, book the dog into the groomer, sort out the groceries for the week. Closing down open tabs in your mind brings inner and outer peace. Try it.

Gaining awareness when I am in resignation and argument with life are the times my own self-care has deteriorated. This could mean a number of things for me, from not having a good sleep, eating crap food, not doing any exercise of movement, or leaving it too long between seeing girlfriends and having a good laugh and share session. Resignation is like a beacon to me to see what is going on inside me. A red flag. It has nothing to do with what is going on outside. It has nothing to do with my family. It is always internal. I will say it again: all answers are within.

STRIPPING IT ALL BACK TO NOTHING.

It was time for me to get clear. I knew clarity was the answer. A huge task. Huge. Taking my heart and mind back to nothing. To strip back everything I had learnt and heard to nothing. Nothing. A fresh sheet of paper. Write a new book for my life.

I got to strip off my amour. To get naked with my soul. To allow the majority of the judgments and opinions of others to go where they needed to go – down the toilet. Throw what society has told me to do as a woman and as a parent in the trash. I was scared. I was clinging on to safety and what I knew. I was also clinging on to knowing that I had to let go. I no longer had a choice. When you feel something in your soul, in your heart, when it has travelled down there it doesn't ever leave. You can put in place whatever coping mechanisms you like. Whatever survival patterns you can dream up. They will work for a period of time. That is probably what a lot of you are doing now. You know how I know, because that is what I did every day. I became a master at it. Avoiding. Numbing. Start this. Start that. Bandaid this. Bandaid that.

One of the scariest questions I had to ask myself was, 'What do I want?' 'What do I, Zoe Martin, at the age of 41, want?' Have you ever done a questionnaire type exercise and it asks, 'What do you like to do?' 'What makes you happy?' 'If you could do anything with your life, what would you do?' 'What are your hobbies?' I have, and at difference points in my life those questions have scared the socks off me. I have frozen, felt ridiculous that I didn't know what I liked to do. That I couldn't answer these questions in 2 seconds with confidence and assertiveness on what I wanted out of life. Imagine being able to create things in your life that you did want instead of creating things that you don't want. Imagine being clear on what you do want. What you want for you and for your family unit. Imagine that. There is a saying that what you focus on grows. You will see that it's true once you start taking steps toward and directing your focus to what you do want. I promise you that.

Stay with me on this one.

We must get clear on what it is we want for ourselves, our kids, our life, our world. Until we figure this out, nothing will change. We will continue to head in any old direction on any old day depending on where we sit in the Dreaded Drama Triangle of Rescuer, Persecutor and Victim. I worked with a guy that had a sign in his office saying, 'If you don't stand for something you will fall for anything'. This has been true for me. If I am not grounded in myself and my mission and what is best for my family and me, I can easily get carried away with what others are doing. We can gain so many ideas from others yet there is a difference in grasping and trying everything from a place of fear and confusion rather than trying and experimenting things from a place of empowerment and confidence.

Taking the next step towards your best self or best life can be scary. Effort and discipline can be required not to slip back into old programming. Courage. Practise and practise and practise. It requires you to be gentle with yourself. It can be a time that is filled with many limiting beliefs and old stories can run wild in your mind. What will others think? I don't know anyone else that wants 'this'. Surely this is selfish, going after what I want. So-and-so's kids don't do this afterschool activity that would be great for my child. What will others think of me filling my cup up? For filling my needs. I'm a mum. You don't put yourself first.

Let me just jump in here and call BS on this 'don't put yourself first' one. I have a lot more to say on this one later. You will begin to question some of your tribe. This can be frightening as most of us feel isolated already. At this stage, it can also be daunting to think that everything you are doing now is your choice. Taking responsibility for yourself requires guts and love. It is a sobering day when you wake up and realise you have created your life.

When you have spent years being a parent, we are generally not in the mindset of asking for what we want. We have also been conditioned to putting ourselves last. If we are in a relationship, we have been conditioned to put that on the back burner while we raise the kids. Conditioned to put our lives on hold until the kids leave home. I can't see any common sense in this mentality at all and I can personally vouch for this conditioning having a detrimental impact on me, my marriage and my children. More on that later.

We can be stuck in the mindset of, 'What do my kids need?' 'What does my partner or other extended family members need?' 'What do my friends need?' 'What does my job need?' Mainly it was my kids and I would constantly ask myself 'What can I do for my kids?'.

A question with ten times the impact is, 'What do I need or want?' The question can be so hard to answer that we avoid it at all costs and keep numbing to avoid answering it. I have been an expert at that during my life. Food consumption and restriction along with over-exercising and recreational drugs were the main numbing tools I started using at 16. I stopped using drugs when I was around 28 years old and stopped binge drinking when I was 30. Alcohol isn't part of my life now. It had been 10 years since I had been drunk and I went to Bali in 2018 and went on a mission to end the draught. It has been on my mind for 3 years. I'm glad I did it. It reminded me that losing control of my mind is not for me. I don't like it. Stopping all those crutches increased my reliance on food and exercise. It went from one thing to another.

Exercise is my happy pill. Finding my balance in this area has brought all those awesome 'happy feels' and is a pressure release for me, in a gentle and positive way. I do some form of movement most days and it is done with love. I move in a way that is conducive for my body. I move because I love it. My mind and body love it. My soul and heart love it. My week of movement could be all planned and I wake up one day and know that what I had planned, isn't the best option for me, so I change it. No guilt only freedom. I may have had limited sleep for all sorts of reasons so doing a big workout isn't what my body needs that day. A walk would be more beneficial for me. Moving is critical to me. It is a non-negotiable yet I can still let it slide (human).

Monkey-see-monkey-do is big in our home. I yell, they yell. I meditate, they meditate. I move, they move. Most of the time. Our kids are active, and we educate them that movement is part of life , just like breathing and eating. Balance. My food journey is a story in itself, and I am entering into a space of using food as fuel and medicine. As nourishment for my mind and body. Am I completely there? So close and where I am is perfect for me right now.

I want to go back to the 'What do I want?' question. Stop for a moment now and ask yourself, 'What do I want?' "How do I want to feel?' Don't freak out. We will get to the kids. It starts with you. Big breaths. Put down the book or phone. Take 3 deep breaths. Ask the question, again. 'What do I want?' How do I want to feel?' Take 3 deep breaths again. What came up for you? All we want to do here is notice what our response is and how we feel in our body. Do you feel tense in your stomach? Does your chest feel open? You may have got 44 different answers from within. You may have got none. There is no right or wrong. Creating awareness of where we are now with this question, is the start.

When I ask myself 'What do I want?', the answers can change a little from time to time. I have 4 main areas I ask this question in – Energy, Family, Work and Love. My consistent answers are:

Energy: I want to feel energetic? from when I wake up to when I go to sleep around 8:30pm. Energy that fuels me to fully show up for myself, my family and the greater good. Energy so I can move, eat and serve at my highest. I want enough energy that I can be intimate with my husband and not be 'too tired'. Energy so I can learn a hip-hop dance that Zhema wants to teach me and play soccer with Billy. Energy so I can catch up with my family and friends. Energy so that I can serve here on earth and fulfil my mission/vision/purpose.

Energy at the kids bedtime to be able to do their sensory work. This is so important to how they sleep. I do a pressure massage and other work on them both, some Reiki if they ask for it and read to them both. If I can't do this for them they take longer to settle and get less sleep. If I am tired, cranky, reactive and ready to fall in a heap then I have not only let myself down but I have let them down. This requires a good night's sleep (this doesn't always pan out, but it is a big part of my life and I have some strict limits around this), food that works for my body and life, daily movement, and meditation topped up with a bucket-load of self-love. Energy is my absolute number 1. Without energy and my health, I cannot live the life that I want. What steps can you take to increase your energy? Start crazy small. What is that one little thing you can start doing today? From this platform the rest will flow. Notice I said start crazy small!

Family: I want to be present with my family. When I mean present, I mean when I am reading to my kids every night at bedtime, I am taking in the story with them and can answer a question if they ask. When I am playing cards with my kids I am focusing on the cards, focusing on them and all the fun family banter (and fights) and not thinking about what we are having for dinner or what needs to be done for work. Present to the point where I see their freckles, notice their tiny ears. See the colour of their eyes when they talk to me and not the front of my phone. Present when my husband talks to me, I stop, drop what I am doing and listen, not just hear. He doesn't talk a lot, and when he does, I now get to really take it in and I take the opportunity of connection. Connection for us looks very different. He doesn't need the amount of connection that I do. Awakening to our differences has brought us closer together and I can rely on my village for connection also. I want to be the best wife and mother that I can be. I want to live with alignment and integrity. I want to live them with an open heart. I am that soft pillow my family can land on at any time.

Work: As each member of my family was diagnosed, I moved from a victim to a woman and mother who knew that she was here on this earth to serve in the Autism space. I want to add value to the world through my voice and my gifts. I want to be there for parents who are on the Spectrum. I want to be there for mothers and fathers who are parenting kids on the spectrum and who are seeking support and clarity on this hero's journey. I provide a support system for parents, someone who they can count on who has gone through the chaos and confusion and found clarity and calm.. Someone who has walked the path and knows that freedom awaits.

Freedom that is unique to each family. Freedom by intentional and conscious design. Someone who has lead her family out of the darkness and into the light. I want parents to realise their children chose them and they are the perfect parent for that child. I remind parents they are human and as humans we experience the full range of emotions, just like their children. I help parents change their predominant state to higher, happier, loving and accepting emotions. I want them to know they are the best parents for their kids. Their kids are the best kids for them. I want kids to know they are not broken and they do not need fixing. I want them to know nothing is wrong. They don't have a disorder. They are a gift. We all are. I want to generate income from a place of love and integrity. I then circulate that money with discernment and support organisations who are making a difference for the greater good. I want to support my family and buy nutritious food and have the money for us to do the activities that light us up. I want money to travel and make memories. I want to invest that money in myself, my family and in projects that serve. I invest that money back in humanity, in you. I am relentless in my self actualisation and I am continuously studying science and modern positive psychology.

Love. In every breath we take we have a chance to return to love. In every breath we take we have a chance to love. To breathe in love and breathe out love. We all drink from the one cup. We have all come from the one source. We are one. I feel we all have the innate need to love and be loved. To love ourselves, to love others, to be loved by others. In August 2018, I flew to America to attend a course from one of my mentors Ivonne Delaflor. I became Australia's first and currently only Transcendental Rebirth Facilitator. Sounds woo woo and yes, some of it is yet it is grounded in modalities that serve humanity – a system that helps you master the use of your central nervous system, access flow & heal in an integrated manner, your family trauma. A modality that can heal and park the past, bring awareness and acceptance to the present (your now) while birthing adults into their brilliant future. The English language fails to do a TR rebirth justice. It was during my own rebirth in America that I accessed the divine love in me. I was seen as me. All of me. In that instant my world changed. I now get to facilitate rebirths and I am so grateful for the outcomes it brings to those that come forth to partake.

In every breath I take I get closer to love. In each action I take I either bring myself further or closer to love. I choose. I also realised I can only love others at the level I love myself. Loving myself is a gift to all. Loving all of me right now in any moment is freedom. Loving everyone exactly where they are at, is where my heart is happy. How quickly I can return to love shows me exactly where I am at.

These big 4 for me are something I reflect on daily. Journaling about my big 4 creates the space to continuously question 'What's important now? (W.I.N.)I am clear on the price I get to pay to bring them into fruition. Focus on what you want, not what you don't want!!! Practise. Practise. Practise. Where your focus goes, energy flows. Focus is a cracker for me. If I am starting to get low on tools, a sure sign is I start to think about the things that I don't want in my life and going back into my past. Examples are that I can start complaining about the kids' behaviour or that I'm not getting enough attention and cuddles from Scott. What happens is the behaviours keep going downhill and I don't get cuddles from Scott. Energy breeds energy, so be mindful where you direct your energy. When we can have an awareness of this, we can then take a big breath and make a choice to shift our focus on to what we do have and what we do want.

Let's start looking at where we are putting our focus, and bring awareness to how we are feeling on a deeper level. This requires practise to check in with our body. To slow down enough to feel, to hear. Meditation is great for this. Journaling is another tool. Quiet. Stillness. See what arises.

When we can slow the mind down enough to hear the heart, magic will happen. There are times in my life where I have committed to something yet I felt anxious doing it. Once I could acknowledge I didn't feel great, I could evaluate the situation. Is this something I was choosing, or is it something I thought was 'right' for me to do by outside opinions or judgements? Big questions to ask oneself!

What is it that you want in your heart, your soul? If you find yourself reacting and not responding, then that may be a sign that you aren't in alignment with this particular choice/focus. An example might be that you want to start going to the gym and doing a weights program. When you go to get ready, you feel a heavy sense of dread. You start to feel your tummy tighten. You push through, telling yourself, 'You are just out of your comfort zone – go and get the workout done.' You get yourself to the gym and start your weights and there is no change in your belly. You aren't enjoying one bit of it. Not one. You finish and get home and you are feeling no better for going. This can be a sign that you are out of alignment with your choice to do weights at the gym.

Another example is you don't want to go, but you get yourself dressed and get to the gym. You are on your second set of bicep curls and you find yourself enjoying the music that you are listening to. You are enjoying the feeling of your muscles contracting and you are looking forward to the last set and how far you can push yourself. You finish your session. You feel better than when you started. You may feel a little flogged depending on your training style, but it is obvious you have received a dopamine bath – you feel it on a cellular level. This is your jam. You just have to get yourself there.

This is when I refer to discipline coming into the equation. That inner knowing that you enjoy something and that it has a positive effect on you. The wisdom to implement it. The wisdom to listen to the voice when it is telling you, 'Go on. You know you will feel better once you get there.' Wisdom is also recognising that weights at the gym isn't your jam as in the first example. That the effect on your mind and body isn't one of a dopamine bath! It is one that raises anxiety and cortisol. Intelligence is being aware you get to find something that is.

Courage is trying something else.

Wisdom is taking action.

There are heaps of opportunities right now where you can take baby steps to start becoming a creator in your life. Choices to make. We always have 2 choices. Sometimes we have numerous choices. Sometimes the choices are minimal. A wise mentor of mine, Emma Barbato said to me many years ago, 'When you say yes to something, you say no to something else.' Each choice you make, you take yourself closer or further. Closer to what you want, or further away from what you want. Closer. Further. You choose. I have the word 'closer' tattooed on my hand as a constant reminder.

It took me a while to really get this concept. Really get that. Every time you do say yes to something, you are saying no to something else. When you say yes to catching up with your girlfriend for a soul chat and cuppa, you are saying no to the housework. When you say yes to eating the whole block of chocolate, big bag of chips, 2ltr tub of ice cream, you are saying no to your health. I have a quote in my bathroom that says, 'There is a price to pay to make things better and there is a price to pay to leave things as they are'.

I am also practicing mastering an honest yes and an honest no. My life has been filled with moments when I have said yes and wanted to say no. Saying no when I was busting to say yes yet I let fear, uncertainty and perfectionism win. I have been blown away by the people I have attracted into my realm once I became aware of this practice. People who say yes and mean it. People who say no with confidence and no guilt. What a way to live!

Becoming a creator is seeing yourself as source. Seeing yourself as the answer. Seeing yourself as the one that is responsible for how you relate to yourself, to others and to life experiences. It is a great thing to ask yourself from time to time – how am I relating? This can be an easy way to catch ourselves out when we have slipped back into victim mode, and trust me, it will happen. We can fall back into being a victim at any time during the day. Multiple times a day. One way I gauge my personal growth is by how quickly I can recognise myself playing the victim and step out of it. There are moments I can step in and out in a matter of seconds. Other times hours. It is all progress and a perfect learning moment.

Creating pockets in your life for introspection brings it all to the surface for unpacking.

I know when I have slipped back into victim mode as I spew out my fears and anxieties on to Scott, I complain and whinge. He is my closest human, along with mum, that I know won't turn their back on me. When I am worried about the kids, I will start nagging Scott. I can nag Scott about 'leaving the clothes sitting in the dryer too long' (really – how about you high-5 the man for doing the washing in the first place?) or coming home after yoga on Sunday mornings and the kids are still in their PJ's (really – how super cool is that for the kids!). You get the picture.

I am looking for any reason to control something in what I feel is an uncontrollable situation. You know what the great thing is? Scott and I are both aware of it, and we can pick this type of scenario up early – talk about it – break it down – take a breath

– and move on fairly unscathed. Don't think that this happens 100% of the time. We still have our heated discussions. There are times when one of us is out of tools, overwhelmed or damn tired and worn down. We are in a constantly evolving bubble and to look back at how far we have come from living in that place of fear, yelling, confusion, shame, blame and guilt, blows my mind and has my heart beating out of my chest with pure joy and gratitude. It is only going to keep getting better from here!

Another example of slipping into victim mode is when the kids both went through a change of medication, one directly after the other. For those of you that haven't gone through this, it can be an emotionally worrying time, to put it mildly. You are going through a change of medication because what they are taking is no longer helping them with their struggles or another major obstacle has presented itself. For us, a change of medication is on the back of hard times all around. Our kids are battling and it's hard. Damn hard on our kids and damn hard as a parent to witness. I remember asking why me? Why us? I was so scared I wasn't enough for what they needed. What was happening with one of our kids at this point was close to our worst nightmare come true.

I won't go in to details as it is one of those times in your life that you think you will wake up soon. That it has to be a dream. That your child is not in this much pain internally. Praying that your worst fear as a parent will not come true. I remember ringing the paediatrician and hanging up the phone and bursting into tears. I could not compute that I had just had a conversation of that nature about my child. I pray no other child or parent has to ever go through it. Ever. For me, it is a time to hang on with all I've got, trust in the universe and village I have, trust in me as their mother and love my child with all I have. Medication is a journey all on its own. It is great to reflect on these times as examples of always being enough. Of always getting through. I remind myself that to date, I have made it through every day. Every day.

Being a Mother and leading a neurodivergent family is many things. For me it is recognising when our kids and husband are in sensory overload and meeting them with acceptance, love and compassion. It is holding space with an open heart. It is not to have an internal sulk when Scott comes home from work and his face shows 100% that he needs space. He needs quiet, to have something to eat, to just sit. He doesn't need me rattling off 888 things that have gone on over the day. I used to take his face personally and think he doesn't even like me. It is not falling into rescuer mode at these times as well. I am not responsible for how my children react or respond. This has been a huge lesson for me to really digest and become comfortable with.

For years, I took my kids behaviour personally. Like it was a direct reflection of my parenting and the way I have bought them up. What I *am* responsible for is the way *I* react and respond, and to be a leader for them. To show them how I self-regulate, how I direct my frustration and anger and how I choose to navigate this thing called life and all the ups and downs that go with it. I am responsible to demonstrate radical love in all that I do.

Previously, I would drop into victim mode as soon as I even smelt the onset of rudeness or a meltdown. I would yell, blame, ridicule, have my own tantrum or numb myself with food. Now I get to step back, evaluate the environment and see what can be implemented. This could be anything from me breathing, giving the kids time and space to have the meltdown, giving them a cuddle, doing nothing at all and letting the yelling and words pass through me, asking some questions about what they need and letting them calm themselves. Sometimes it is all of that. To be in this headspace, I have to pay close attention to how I am feeling and keep tabs as to where my cup is at. I have to take responsibility for me.

I get to check in with my central nervous system.

Again and again and again. And again.

I get to create how I am in any moment.

My choice.

I choose.

I get to take radical responsibility for my actions.

The great and the not so great.

We can either choose to respond or react. Big difference.

Responsibility: the ability to respond. I have this word written in café neon pen on my bathroom mirror. It says Responsibility = Respond = Love. We get to choose if we meet their anger with anger. If we meet their yelling with yelling. Remembering we are human.

Chapter 4...

NOURISH THE NOURISHER.

We are wired to love our kids. Our kids are wired to love us back. At night, when my kids get into bed, my hearts nearly bursts with a love that only a mother knows. I often talk to my kids after they have had a situation where they aren't feeling great about themselves. It could be after an anger outburst. I tell them that there is nothing they can ever do or say that would make me stop loving them. Nothing. Ever.

I feel their hearts soften. I feel their souls relax. I feel them open into my love. I tell them that I am proud of them in this life that can be hard. I remind them how I feel good in my belly when I hang out with them. I tell them they are funny and make me laugh (we tell the worst funniest jokes at the Martin Castle). I share that sometimes just having a crack is all you need to do. I tell them that some things we can get perfect and others we can't, yet they can still stand back and high-5 themselves for their efforts. I tell them that showing up is the result.

Perfectionism can be strong in Autistic kids and adults and can cause a lot of anxiety. I know this first hand. Seeking perfection! Over achiever! Stuck in toxic doing! I got in and out. How would your life be different if you said these positive and understanding words to yourself? Yep, yourself. How would your life be different if you made sure you moved your body and got a certain amount of activity and 'off screen time' like we try to get our kids to do? I now have 1 day a week of no phone/technology. I am hoping to move it to 2. It is bliss. Absolute bliss. And I think it is a great thing to model to our children. What if you tried to make the best food choices for you like we try to make for our kids, so they run at their optimal levels? We are going to dive into the self-love conversations. Why? Because like the old saying goes, on the aeroplane you need to put your own oxygen mask on first, before you can help anyone else.

Depending where you are on this journey of diversities with your child will likely govern the conversations you are having with yourself. Trust me, the further you get along, the more you can focus on you first, the more nourishing and enabling those conversations with yourself are going to be. Did I just say focus on you first? What? Am I mad? Nope, that wasn't a typo. It is my truth. You can get all the therapy and intervention for your child that you can afford, access and fit into your life, but if you are a mess internally then all that support is only going to have a certain impact. I guarantee you that your child will not be able to implement all the tools, tips and practices if you aren't running close to your awesome self most of the time. Notice how I said most of the time. Surely that now confirms I am not mad. If I said 100% of the time, I would close the book now and ask for a refund!

This is a tricky time. It can be an emotional, confusing and terrifying time. It can also be the time in your life where you take back your identity, create your family's own blueprint and take the path to freedom! Your freedom! We have a few hats to wear. They could include Mother, Partner, Daughter, Friend, Aunty, Business Owner, Employee… the list goes on. Now is the time to get clear about what is important in your life and what you now let go of. Maybe you let them go forever or maybe you let them go for the time being. To me, what was important was myself, my husband and my children. Everything after that went through a priority and feeling odometer. Spreading yourself thinly is a fast track way to burnout, exhaustion, brain-fry and confusion. Trying to be everything to each of those hats is not going to work. Trust me. I did it and it led to a downward spiral of my physical and mental health. The downward spiral of me.

Now you get to write your own story for the direction of your life. I had to make choices about my time and with whom and what I did with it. Going out for hours and hours doesn't serve my family unit. That is a clear decision we now make around our family. We are a family that goes to bed early and rises early so staying out late doesn't work for us either. It is a joke between my girlfriends that if we are going out for dinner it has to start early so I am home in bed at 8:30pm. For me, it's a non-negotiable, and I say no to some things as I just know I won't get home until late. Do I miss out on things. Yes. Does missing out create the life I desire. Yes. This is a great example of me saying yes to my energy and vitality and no to feeling like crap the next day.

So, how do us mums look after ourselves? Where do we find the time? I have worked in the finance industry for 25 years, ending in having a mortgage broking business. I know what long hours are. I know what working 24/7 means. I know what it is like to spend weeks on end at the hospital with one premmie baby while you have another baby at home. I know what it is like to get 2 kids to therapy appointments. To paediatrician appointments. To keep track of who has done a poo today and who hasn't. To go to out and realise your child has grown and that one pair of joggers they have, no longer fit and it's a jogger wearing event.

I know what it's like to be in charge of all the family administration and money along with running two businesses. I know what it's like to have kids sick, your husband has to go to work, and it's up to you to juggle work and the kids. I know what it is like to go to an important business meeting, have the kids porridge on your black pants and have only one high heel in the car! I know what it's like to be unhappy with your appearance and to have let yourself go because you made excuses and 'don't have the time'. I know what it is like to fall into bed at the end of the day, cry yourself to sleep praying that tomorrow is a better day.

I know what it is like to just want one day to yourself or just one hour of peace and quiet. I know what it is like to want to run away from it all. For ever.

On the flip side, I know what it takes to set boundaries without feeling like you are letting people down. I know what it feels like to honour those boundaries and the inner calm and peace that awaits. People pleasers feel like they let people down. Women who are making decisions for themselves and their family don't feel 'bad' for doing so. They are grounded in their 'why'. They are confident in their decisions. They know they are worth it and so is their family. They know that by saying an honest no to something, they are saying an honest yes to themselves. They know they live from a place of love.

Self-care is a word that has a different meaning to everyone. Now I prefer to use self-love. That resonates with me and for me, the level of self-care I gift myself is directly impacted by my level of self-love. What ever it means to you and what ever it looks like for you is going to differ to me. This is because our kids are all at a different ages and abilities and we have attached a story to what we can and can't do for ourselves at this point in life. It can also be because we all have a different village supporting us. Some have none. We all have a different level of self-worth. Self-care can be a whole lot of little things that send a message to your heart that you are worthy. That you appreciate you. A message that you are super important. So loved. So epic. Now. We all operate within unique constraints. All of us.

You get to find your own flexible and logical way to get what you need.

These little things can be waking up 15 mins earlier and washing your face. Making a cup of tea and taking some deep breaths or staring into space before the house wakes up. It could be gently stretching your body. It could be texting a girlfriend and catching up for coffee. It is having your pap smear, skin and breast checks. It could be asking for someone to look after your child so that you can go for a walk. It could be hugging a tree and feeling the wisdom of mother nature.

These are all messages to yourself that you care.

I am at the point in my life where my self-care comes first. I have created that and chosen self-care as my number one weapon. Nourish the nourisher. Number one. Do my plans work out every day perfectly? No. Not at all. Do I fit some form of self-care in daily? 100%. For me, self-care is journaling and declaring what I am grateful for in my life and doing a brain dump. It is going to a Pilates or yoga class or walking the dog. It is getting up, meditating and stretching before the kids wake up. Prioritising getting the kids looked after for 2 hours and going for coffee with my husband. Having a bath when I can (which normally means running the bath, letting the kids get in first then I get the bath last – I don't complain). It is the intention to meditate daily. Self-care is watching a movie/documentary once a month on the

TV (I'm not into watching the TV – even as a kid I didn't watch it much) and enjoying just sitting there.

Self-care is getting into bed at night and reflecting on the day and all the moments I showed up in life. One of my favourite activities is being in mother nature. Laying on the green grass and being held by mother earth. Walking through the trees and along the beach near where I live. Waking up early on a Sunday and watching the sun rise when I feel like it. Mother nature has helped heal my heart. She shows me daily how effortless she is in her beauty and love. She shows me how sometimes you just gotta let it all out and go again.

Self-care enables me to serve at my best. Self-care is being able to invest and work on my passion and mission, which is coaching/guiding/supporting mothers and fathers through the inner and outer chaos and confusion that can come with parenting kids on the spectrum. Awakening parents to their inner wisdom. Awakening their hearts. I help mothers get to the core of what they want in their life. Unpacking their life and shining a spotlight on what is and isn't working. Implementing tools, strategies that are proven and work. Accountability ensures the transformations are sustainable. Mothers feel heard, seen and deeply supported. I help them unpack so that clarity and calm can be reached. Living a life with smiles and confidence is her predominant state. All this applies to Dads also. She matters. He matters. Together they matter.

When it comes to time, it is about making time. I know some of you don't want to hear that we all have the same amount of time in a day. Fact – we do. Let's take the focus off the old 24 hours in a day trick and look at a 7-day week. There is 168 hours in a 7-day week. Saying you don't have time for self-care is like saying you don't have time to breathe. To me, you might as well be dead. Self-care is going to look differently for all of us. It might look like scrolling through Instagram or trekking up a mountain. It might be having a glass of wine or 2 while watching Netflix for 3 hours. It might be sitting at the traffic lights and taking 3 deep breaths. It could be shaving your legs and armpits (a big high-5 if you get them done at once!). It might be having a sleep while your child sleeps. It might be cleaning the house.

So, how do you find the time? You make it. Simple. No scientific equations. No magic potion. You can't buy it. You can't install an app on your phone and push a button. You make a conscious choice that you are important. You make it work. You put it in your calendar. Yes, I do live on planet earth and in reality. I am human, and life is going to happen along the way. Kids get sick. Kids are in sensory overload and you get to be there to help them through the morning or afternoon, and that takes up the time you had allocated for you. Work gets super busy. Our end game is that we have a self-care buffer, so when life does happen our bucket isn't completely empty, and we can carry on fairly unscathed until the next opportunity arises. It is when we are depleted physically and mentally and then the unexpected happens and we miss our window and you know what will hit the fan.

You are like a time bomb ticking, then tick tick tick boom! We have all been there. I used to be an expert at it. Put everyone else first. Take the kids to this that and the other thing at the sacrifice of myself. Not go to yoga or Pilates on Sunday morning because I would feed myself the story that the kids should be able to wake up to a mum and dad on a Sunday. What is the point of that if mum is a nut case? None. Zero. Zilch. Zip. Nil. No one wins.

What my kids need is a mum who radiates from her heart, a mother that loves herself, her family and the universe. They need a mum who looks after herself physically and mentally, so she can show up for them when she is home. What is better – a mum that is home 24/7 that is unhappy and disconnected from herself and her kids? Or a mum who, when she is home, she is loving life, ready to engage and connect with her kids and can handle the messy moments of parenting kids on the spectrum with grace? No-brainer for me. I have a self-care buffer built into my life, and so can you. It takes work and you guessed it, practise!

I explain the buffer like a bicycle wheel. You start with a wheel with all the spokes intact. The wheel functions to perfection. Your self-care cup is full. It is Friday, and you miss going for a walk which you love to do, and it is a positive activity for your body and mind. One spoke breaks. No problem. Your wheel still turns like a dream. Your bike is at its full function. It's lunchtime Sunday and you are staaarrrrvvving, and coming back in the car from seeing family and your car drives into fast food drive thru and you order a burger meal. Amazing how cars can just drive themselves into a fast food joint. No big deal, except it is the third time this week. 3 burger meals are not going to fuel that human suit to keep you running at a level that is going to bring positive loving change to your life. Fact. Now you are 4 spokes down.

If you could visualise now that the bicycle wheel has 4 out of 20 spokes snapped. The durability and strength of that wheel has become compromised. A few more 'out of integrity moments' and a few more spokes broken. The collapse of your wheel is inevitable! You won't be riding your bike. You will more than likely be frustrated, agitated, short fused, playing the victim, blaming or hating on yourself and not being the woman that your heart knows you can be.

Monday morning comes, and life happens; you have a meeting with the school and that means you cancel the catch up with your girlfriend that your soul so needs. 8 spokes down. Then comes the clanger that tips you over as you have no buffer – your child is having a tough time sorting out what needs to be done on this school morning. They have woken up a little off – you sense it and you see it in their face instantly, let alone that they walked out of their bedroom clearly out of tools before anyone had even looked at them. You have asked the child 6 times to get dressed, then tick tick tick boom. You lose it. You look at the clock. You have 8 minutes before you have to get in the car. Time got away as you were running around doing 333 things like you can do on a morning when sensory overload is in full swing. You can't ride your bike. Your wheel is literally broken. Bent out of shape. It won't physically go round and round. Breakdown. You lose your bananas. This then sets your child off. It is now time to get in the car.

Years ago, some school mornings it would end up with all 3 of us crying. I would explode, they would cry and then I would cry. I had no buffer. I also didn't know what I didn't know. We would gather ourselves and I would drop them off to school and think of all the energy they had used up from me not being able to look after myself and my emotions. I would think of how precious that wasted energy was for them to be able to navigate the day. Energy they needed to hold themselves together in front of their peers. Energy they needed to do what the teacher asked.

These reasons here along with many others were what my heart kept telling me in my quiet moments: *Zoe – it starts with you.* It starts with loving yourself enough to look after yourself first.

I was thinking yesterday while I was driving about this self-care chapter. Our kids get all the help and therapy and attention. Society deems a good mother is one who gets them to their appointments and gets them to play with the therapy putty to build strength in their fingers to help their writing. We help them write the number 3 the right way and to talk about the zones of regulation and feelings. We role play social situations to help them make friends. We seem to down play the importance of doing what is best for ourselves. The importance of reconnecting the wiring to our wisdom and intuition that seems to have been severed through the diagnosis journey. Time and effort at the start is required to make self-care a given. Practise. Practise. Practise. Just do it. When you can, the best you can. The wheel buffer analogy can be used when it comes to integrity and responsibility, too. Be mindful of it. Take notice of when your integrity and responsibility is breaking down. Build it up before it blows out and breaks down.

So, how do we build up a reserve of self-care when we are only surviving now? Little by little, my friend. Little by little. We start small. Can we pack up today and go to a retreat for a month? No. Can we start by talking kindly to ourselves? Yes. Can we start to notice in our lives where we are wasting our precious time and where we could be doing something that sets our soul alive? Something that brings a smile to our face. Can we notice when 'this' no longer feels good for us.

Social media can be a big-time waster for me. There is so much good stuff on social media, and I love lovelove it, but there are also times where I just mindlessly scroll and scroll and scroll and I know I could be doing something way more beneficial for me. This is where I get to call bs on myself. If my cup is going ok then I could be cooking dinner, so the arvo/nighttime shift is calmer, and I can be there for the kids and playing a friendly family game of UNO (UNO can get quite competitive in our house!) or a game of handball. I could take the dog for a walk. I could do some jobs so the weekend isn't as crazy, therefore creating some self-care moments when that time comes. Social media can drain our life and fry our brain if we let it.

If you are a parent that doesn't have a lot of support, then we get to look into what you do have. As you go through your days and while you are doing this or that, you can ask yourself – is this completely necessary to be done now (or at all), and is this an opportunity where I could just sit, breath and smile for 3 minutes at the fact that to date I have a 100% success rate of getting through a day? Once you have an awareness of where your time is going, you can then look at ways you can chop things out and add things in. This is one of my gifts that I am very passionate about. Helping mothers implement self-care strategies that see them access happiness.

There have been long snippets of time where Scott and I didn't do much together at all because we weren't comfortable leaving the children. Anything we did, we did separately. He would go to golf. I would look after the kids. I would go out with friends and he would look after the kids. Having 2 kids on the spectrum with different needs and clashing makes it extra tricky at times. It is hard enough for Scott and me as their parents to navigate at times, let alone someone who doesn't live it 24/7. We have been blessed with bits of time away on our own along the way. We have had a night away maybe once a year. We have a few people who can help us here and there. We don't go out that much, as parenting kids on the spectrum and keeping your self-care up and self-regulation at optimal levels can be tiring. We do what works for us and what makes us happy.

We have never been away for 2 nights in a row on our own. Scott and I didn't have a honeymoon. We had some things going on in my family and it wasn't the right time to get away. We are planning to build up over the next few years to have a 4 night getaway. My goodness. Imagine that. Yeah, baby!!! Life goals right there. Bring it on!! Thank the universe for family (for my family reading this – stay tuned for save the dates to enjoy my treasures!!!).

My self-care toolbox is a big one, and here are the things I do that I love:

Climb Mt Ngungun – I love this mountain. It is a mountain that my kids can climb too, and that gets them out into mother nature. I take them once or twice a year. I do it on my own a lot. It brings me great peace and holds many messages for me. Each time I climb it I get a new message from her. I get the standard ones like – just put one foot in front of the other, just like in life – you choose where you put your feet, just like in life – pay attention to where you are walking or you just might trip, just like in life. Mother nature is my biggest healer outside of myself. I connect with her in some form every day. I came from her and I will return to her.

Coffee shops and Journaling – I love to go to the coffee shop and order my almond latte. It is a gift to me for being Godzilla Epic at this mothering game. I love a coffee on my own and journaling. I love to work and write at coffee shops. Journaling has so many benefits. It is a ritual that is very precious to me. I also love a coffee with my husband and with my friends. I seem to do my best work at coffee shops including the writing of this book.

Bath – I love to have a bath with Epsom salts and essential oils. I light a candle and lay back. Yes, I can hear the goings on of the house and I smile. Yes, the kids come in and talk to me and I smile. It is only really the last 6 months that I have been having baths. I have had the odd one since having kids. You could count them on 2 hands in 9 years. I am now carving out time for them as I know how they make me feel. Sometimes, at night, I would ring my mum and she would be in the bath or reading a book and I would say in shock horror, 'What – you are reading a book?' or 'What – you are having a bath?' like that just wasn't a normal thing to do. Now, I am having a bath, reading or listening to audio books.

Walking – walking soothes my heart, body and mind. I love trees and the water, and I am blessed to live where a path leads through trees and to the water. Sometimes I take the dog, sometimes I take the kids, but I always carve out time for just me to walk. Sometimes I listen to books, podcasts or music, and a lot of the time it is silence. Sometimes I talk to myself, and most of the time you will see me walking along, smiling from ear to ear, looking out at mother nature and bowing to her with my soul. You will also see me hugging a tree. Walking is gentle on the body. It doesn't send my cortisol through the roof. It gets my blood pumping. I can control if I want to walk briskly or slowly, or both. Walking is healing for me and creates space in my head.

Laying on the grass – grounding – is something I do often. I aim to do it daily. Sometimes 30 seconds, sometimes longer. Grounding is having part of your body directly touching the earth and receiving the negative ions. When I am touching the earth, something happens on a cellular level. I feel it. I let the ground hold me and support my body. I am big on getting the kids to take their shoes off at any opportunity and get their feet on the grass. Science is proving the lack of contact kids are having with the ground is directly affecting their brains' and bodies' and behaviour. Think back to the 'olden days' and how much kids would be getting around with no shoes on and touching the earth. Google it – grounding on the earth. Mind blowing.

Yoga, Pilates & Stretching – these are my true loves when it comes to moving my body (along with walking). What a gift to give your body. For me, these methods of movement serve me well. In these environments I am safe and there are always options for me to take depending on how my body is at the time. When it comes to moving your body, I always say do what you love.

Going to the beach – I've loved the beach since I was a little girl. It still soothes my soul. Something about the sand on my feet. As a kid we would go sailing on my Dad's yacht. Swimming in the ocean is like having an aura cleanse – washing away what doesn't serve me and bringing me the freshness of the new. We like to camp a few times a year at the beach. I am creating awesome family memories along the way. I am lucky the kids and Scott love it too.

Lighting a candle and incense – this simple act brings me joy. Watching the flame and smoke is a form of meditation for me. A ritual of presence.

Markets on a Sunday – I love going to my local markets on a Sunday after yoga or pilates. Especially in the cooler months. The mornings are so crisp and clear. The kids have pancakes, have a jump on the jumping castle, Scott and I grab a coffee or 2 and we get our raw honey and fruit and veg. It brings me a sense of community.

Connecting with my girlfriends. No words needed.

Connecting with my favourite Buddhist monk, Dondrub.

Watching the sunrise and sunset – I try and catch the sunrise on a Sunday when I can. It signals to me the start of new beginnings – another day. A blank canvas for me to create the day I choose. One thing I love about camping is the sunrises and sunsets. At home I can see the colours of the sun rising and setting. It is another moment where I thank mother nature for her beauty. We live close to Woody Point, and it is said to have one of the best sunsets in the world. I'm certainly not well-travelled, but it takes my breath away every time I see it. Every now and then we head down to the park there and grab fish and chips for dinner on the weekend and watch the sunset. Magic moments.

Gardening – I love all things plants and dirt. I don't do much gardening at the moment. I am slowly increasing it. Little by little. A great way to get your kids outside and dirty! They love it! One of the greatest memories I have is when the kids and I built a Fairy Garden with succulents and crystals. It has a big porcelain Strawberry house and a big Broccoli that is a gym for Fairies. It was one of those moments a few years ago that the kids worked together without fighting. They helped each other and workshopped the design and everyone had a voice, and everyone listened. We all laughed and had so much fun. It was probably the first time that had happened. Facilitating things like that with 2 kids on the spectrum can be like trying to pick up a cactus. Although you do your best, you are going to get pricked!

Having a cuddle with Scott - this is self-care for me. Cuddling isn't something that has come natural to Scott the way it does to me. He is wired to cuddle his kids as their father. Hugs and cuddles are my favourite thing in the world when it comes to physically expressing emotion. I do love a High Five too. We have a Free Hug station in our house that Zhema created. Now that Scott and I know what page we are on, I ask him for a hug or cuddle and he gives me one. I used to resent the fact that I had to ask in the first place, and thought it was a reflection of how he felt about me. That couldn't be further from the truth. He has done a 180 degree turn around in this area, and there is the odd day that he will ask if I want one.

Yep, after 20 years, give or take. Now we can openly discuss our wiring and talk about our wants and needs, he is working super hard to remember that touch is something that I would like – not just when you know what is on the cards. I am working super hard to gift him space and quiet. I cuddle and hug my kids a lot. I breath them in. I feel them in my heart. Sometimes my love for them feels so enormous in my body that launch at them unexpectantly with some kind of touch.

Seeing my family – I have the most amazing family. I am lucky that they all live in pretty close proximity to me. I see my mum often. When I do see my brothers and their families there is lots of smiles, jokes and hugs going on. Thank goodness for smart phones, FaceTime, the crazy messenger photos you can take now, and good old video. Team Martin pride ourselves in the fun videos that we do for our family! My family means the world to me.

Listening to an audio book or podcast – how good is this era we live in? Wow. I can be cruising along doing my mum jobs and listening to a podcast or book. A-mazing. This must have been invented by a busy woman. A podcast that I tribute to keeping my head above water in these early years on the road to diagnosis is TiLT. Mum discovered it, and without a doubt I would listen to a podcast every day. Some I would listen to over and over again. Debbie has a son, Asher, who is on the spectrum, and she shares from her heart her own experiences and has hands down the most insightful guests on her show. Check it out. You are welcome. She has also just launched a book, *Differently Wired*, which I am yet to read. It has come out on audio so I'm in luck!

Meditation – Meditation is a gift to your entire being. There are so many ways to mediate and you can Google the benefits of it. There are about 4 billion benefits. Just listening to music can be a form of meditation. Single pointed focus. Focusing on the music and bringing your mind back when it wonders. It will. You are human. Mediation can also be when you are in the shower and focusing on the water running down your face or back. It can be standing in the check-out line at the grocery store and taking 3 big breaths and focusing on your breathing. I could write a whole book on the benefits/power of breath. It is one of your greatest weapons in this life. 100%. An epic tool in your toolbox and it is free!

If you don't know what you like, try something new. Listen to a podcast. Download a book. Grab a friend and go for a walk in a new location. Walk fast, walk slow. See how it feels. As you go about your day, take notice of when you are feeling good in your belly. In your gut. In your heart. Notice when your face smiles. Do more of that!

Self-care is 100% your responsibility. Self-care is sacred to you. Don't get caught up in what that other mum is doing. Take note of what she is doing as a way of gathering ideas. Gathering data. Remember, laying on your back and doing absolutely nothing is self-care too!

I promise that if you start looking after yourself life will start to change for the better. I promise. Sometimes we have to put our hand up and say, 'Hey! I need some help!' Sometimes we might have to send a text to a friend and ask them to come over and look after our kids while we get out of the house for an hour. Sometimes, we will need to think outside the box on how we can carve out some time. If you are feeling overwhelmed or you can hear yourself saying, 'Zoe has no idea about my life!', then that is a sure sign that you need some self-care. Start with 1 minute. Start small and build from there. Do it. You are worth it. You will thank yourself for it. Your kids will thank you for it (maybe not now, but they certainly will later when you are showing up in life).

Chapter 5...

The Men in your child's life, your life, and being married to a man on the Spectrum.

Let's clear something up now – the role of a male in your child's life is a critical one.
My opinion.

This whole book is based on my opinions, experiences of my own, experiences of people that have shared their stories with me and how I perceive the majority. I won't keep saying 'my opinion' now that we have cleared that up. Moving on.

Male role-models/carers are just as important as female role-models/carers. We all have the masculine and feminine energy in all of us, and by having great role-models and carers we learn how to balance these energies, along with our children learning to balance them – yin and yang. From my experience, the males in my life bring a different perspective, and I am grateful with every cell in my body for those 'other eyes' to see through. The males in my life are very masculine and have a fairly high level of black and white thinking – Scott tops the list on the black and white thinking! I haven't always felt so open to seeing their side. It wasn't until I opened my heart, put my ego and judgement to the side that the lines of communication really opened up in my marriage that I could truly listen, hear and contemplate Scott's side of things, let alone implement and realise that his opinions were so valid and of great use both with my life and the kids.

The male and female brains are wired differently. Our brains are different. I read that famous book *Men are from Mars and Women are from Venus* about 20 years ago. The title says it all. Different planets, people. Different planets. I would often say that I found it comical that we were created so differently and then expected to share a habitat, raise children and live in harmony. Mmmm, the harmony didn't happen straight up for Scott and me and creating it is an ongoing process. I hope you can learn something from my story, so that you won't spend any more years on opposite teams.

I spent most of our relationship controlling everything. My career in finance was based on deadlines and due dates. There were people on the other end of the deadlines and due dates with big emotions and I honoured that. I lived by the clock. I was in a feminine role while I was in conversation with the clients, then a very masculine role behind the scenes. I took that masculine role home with me. I thought I knew what was best for the kids.

I would dismiss Scott and his input. I went to a Steve Biddulph talk a couple of years ago and he spoke of the female taking over the household and the damage of what it was doing – especially to our boys. It hit me like a knife in my heart. If you ever get the opportunity to see either Steve or Maggie Dent talk – go. Thank me later.

If you can, stop here and think how my behaviour made Scott feel amongst everything we had going on with the kids. Talk about hit a man while he is down. I was winning at that game and that is a game I now don't choose to play. The hit to his ego. To his heart. To his intuition and wisdom that he was drawing on as a father. As a human with a right to speak his truth. I was so closed off that I couldn't see that I was taking over some of his roles in the home as well. Stripping him of his masculinity while stripping me of my femininity was destroying our marriage little by little. While I was controlling and masculine, I wasn't able to relax and feel my femininity.

To be able to relax enough to be fully intimate in the bedroom was a rare thing back then and it still can be difficult for me. Being disconnected mentally and physically from your partner, if you have one, has a direct flow-on effect to the children, too. They feel this unseen energy. The kids feel the love, respect and support we now have for each other. They see us having a heated discussion and how we untangle that in a healthy way. Their behaviour has changed because of it. The majority of the time we now hold space and listen without judgement. Listen. It has taken Scott and I years and years to get to where we are now. Where I can talk and share, and he can listen and not feel he has to 'fix' anything. Where he can talk and share, and I can see his side of things.

A male loves to fix fixfix, and that is one of the reasons I have found they struggle so much through this whole journey with the journey of having children on the spectrum. They can't fix Autism because there is nothing to fix. There is nothing broken. What is before them is a child running a different software system that needs their understanding. Needs them to parent from a new direction. A child that needs their radical love and an open heart. Not a fixing attitude. A child whose brain is crying out for support. A child who needs to be loved, just as they are. Every day. A child desperate to be accepted.

The male mind is telling them something is wrong, and they are left feeling useless and confused. Their child can be a mirror for them and that mirror can raise all sorts of stories, trauma and pain from their past. That mirror can also create immense fears and feelings of inadequacy. On top of that, add me who is making him feel unheard, not needed, and left out. I would shut down on him. He wouldn't even want to speak to me. I would not want to speak to him, either. This is how we lived in those dark days.

Out of fear and trying to sort our kids out, old school parenting got a big run in the lead-up to the diagnosis as a final way of trying to fix it once and for all. Especially with Billy. It was a 100% fail. Parenting Billy front on is not an option. It just isn't. His wiring with authority is based on fairness (from his perspective). If you hit him, he will hit you back. If you yell at him, he will yell back. Try and get an old school parenting mind around this and watch it erupt like a volcano. 100% of the time.

Our paediatrician and his psychologist at the time would tell Scott time and time again that this is an Autism trait that Billy has. Billy is not being disrespectful on a personal level to Scott. This is something that Scott still battles with at times. He has come to a 90% realisation of this. Huge. It was a 0% realisation at the beginning. All our own social conditioning takes time and patience to unlearn. The way we were parented or not parented. Be gentle with yourself and others in your life as you all discover your own truth. I have said that Billy is that person in this life that will call me out on my own stuff. Every time. Guaranteed. I get away with nothing and I love him for it. This is another reason I have those conversations with Billy about who I am becoming. It is like a free live-in coach for me! Love him for it (along with his ability to remember things – places – events!!!)

One of the big things we discovered with parenting kids running Autistic/ADHD/ADD/PDA wiring is that old school parenting has no place in our home. The majority of the men that I have come across are wired for old school parenting. For most, that is what they know from their own childhood. Whether it worked for them or not, it is what they know, and how society to a large degree expects them to raise their children. I feel a big shift in humanity and expectations around this. When the mother goes first and shows a different way to do things, the father can see the results and benefits and that gives him confidence to lean into his fears and 'give it a go'.

Our family thrives on clear boundaries, coaching not parenting, and returning to love as soon as we can. Our kids need sherpas – not parents. The road to this realisation was painful. It was really dark at times. Traumatic. It was nights sobbing myself to sleep while Scott would hold me and tell me we were doing our best and that we would work it out. I was running the story on replay that I was messing my kids' lives up and the damage I was causing would be permanent. I was running lots of stories in my head that were not true. They were based on fear. It hurt. It hurt so much that I felt the pain physically. I would feel it in my solar plexus. I would feel it in my throat. My jaw would ache from clenching it so much. The physical pain was nothing compared to the emotional pain.

We were doing the best we could with the tools we had. I will repeat, when you don't know, you don't know. It is time to forgive yourself. I hope that by reading this book it will save you spending the amount of time we did in this 'old school will fix it' phase.

Life on the other side of 'old school', lived with forgiveness for the past and moving forward with an open mind and heart, is filled with moments that are so good you will struggle at first to find words to do them justice. You will have moments when you sit there holding your child and they are thanking you for always looking after them, for always being there for them, for all the times they felt they didn't deserve your love and you showered them in it.

Now back to males…

One of my passions is bringing the male and female together in a container that is filled with a new level of acceptance for our differences. This is a passion of mine because of where Scott and I were all those years ago and where we are today. I know it is possible. I know what waits for you on the other side. I know what it takes to get there. You will eat many surrender sandwiches, my friend. Many. And they start out tasting like the worst sandwich you have ever had and grow into the sandwich from that shop that nails it. Here we embrace understanding. We cultivate acceptance around the way we give and receive love, the way we express our feelings, the way we each require different ways of self-care, of validation… the list goes on.

Communication is where it is at.

Crystal clear communication from your heart. Take a deep breath, get out of your mind, drop into your heart and speak. From my experience, it has been the females who lead the charge in this area. I have found that once I worked out the way I wanted to be loved, the way I wanted to be treated, the way I wanted to spend any time that I got to myself, then I could communicate that to Scott, and that opened the door for him to communicate back. If only you could see me years ago and the torture and turmoil I put myself through because I didn't understand our love languages. Because I didn't understand that males need to protect, provide and fix.

Communicating what you want and working together to do what you can to get everyone's needs met has changed the trajectory of my life. My family's life.

This doesn't just apply to romantic relationships. Crystal clear communication applies to all of our relationships. Especially your children. Our children want to feel that their needs are super important to you. What they want to do matters. Can we buy a horse, jump on a plane to Disneyland today or eat 58 cookies in a row? No – yet we can still validate and hear their requests. Communicating together you can work out a compromise like go for a horse ride, put Disneyland on the dream list and eat 57 cookies.

Conversation around how they would like you to respond when they are angry. Do they want you to wait on the floor by their bedroom door when they are screaming 'Get out"? Do they want you to say 'I love you. I'm here whenever you are ready for a hug.' then leave them (this is what my daughter has asked I do at the moment and check on her every 5 minutes)? Work out what you want – ask what the other person wants – work out how you can both make that happen. If the other person doesn't know what you want, then how are they supposed to even try to deliver? I will let you in on a secret: I thought Scott could read my mind until a few years ago. Here is another secret: speak up.

One common theme that I have discovered along the way is that a father will often say, 'There is nothing wrong with him/her,' or 'It's all in your mind,' or 'What would the teacher know,' or 'All boys do that,' or 'She is no different to such-and-such', 'You are overacting, I can't see that. Who have you been speaking to?'. I reckon I have heard hundreds of one liners passed on from mothers I have worked and spoken with, and Scott came out with a few crackers himself. I have found that most fathers don't see what mothers see. We seem to be switched on to a frequency that looks more closely and really notices the not-so-obvious things. Maybe it is just that we are wired to hear that little voice in our heads saying… 'Mmmm, that was interesting, what my daughter just did…' 'Mmmm, did he really just react like that to me saying no?…' 'Mmmm, why does she keep doing that?…' Where I feel men are more wired to think the child is defiant, out of control, disrespectful, ill-mannered and generally don't see the same things we see.

No one is right or wrong. It is just different and different is ok.

I found myself resenting Scott for not seeing what I saw. If he literally didn't see it in the first place or didn't see it in the same way as I did, I would get so mad. Our communication skills were poor and we weren't going anywhere, and neither were the kids.

This is certainly a big contributor to the length of time it took for the diagnosis to unravel in my house. Resentment breeds victim mentality and disconnection. Once you move into the space of respect, acceptance of difference and love, all this goes away, and you are left with a relationship that is placed in the perfect position for your child regardless of whether you are with the other parent or not.

Learning when and how to drop information about your child to the male in their life is huge. This can be a massive factor for your child in getting the support, nurturing and help they need from both carers. I have been blessed with a husband who had the courage to get an assessment, and in turn I was given a labelthat changed the course of our marriage. His diagnosis paved a way for me to do things differently, to pause, evaluate the day, the timing, the amount of information that I hand over, whether it is best hearing this from me or the professional/therapist. Telling Scott about a social or behavioural difference our child is having needs to be dropped at the right time for him, not me. If I tell him when it suits me, then I run the risk of him not being able to fully receive it. I would risk him becoming defensive immediately. Constructive conversations, not arguments.

Two grown adults communicating like adults who care greatly for the child being discussed. Adults who care for each other. Adults who can stop and say, 'Thanks. That is a lot for me to take in and I am going to need time to process it.' And the other person can say, 'Cool. Let me know when you are ready to chat about it again.' I'm serious. This is all possible. This is our reality. Do we still disagree and have to agree to disagree? Yes.

It is rare that we come to this point, but it does happen. Do we raise our voice and get defensive and spew out our own fears? Yes. We return to love and are able to express what just happened for us. Returning to love is something we speak about often in our home. It started with Scott and me. When we are shut down, angry and defensive, no one is winning. The sooner we can return to love, the sooner we all win. It is like a pendulum – down and back up to balance. Having Autism wiring can fire that amygdala and keep us in these lower vibrating states for a lot longer. It takes practise and courage to step out and back into love. Try it. It is worth it. Every Time. We talk about this with the kids as well. Staying angry and resentful doesn't help them. Calming their minds and bodies so their hearts can open again is something we value and model.

My best advice if you have a male who is defensive about your child's differences and diversities is to be patient. Give them time. Be gentle. They love that child as much as you do. Do what you can while they process it. Lead from the front. I said before, Mothers go first. Go first. There was a fair period of time when I had ditched the old way of parenting and was following my inner wisdom and intuition along with the tips and tricks from professionals, therapists, what I had researched and other mothers, and Scott wasn't up to where I was. I would yell at Scott if he yelled at the kids. Yep, yell at him to stop yelling at the kids.

My lioness would roar, and I would yell before I even realised. I wanted to protect my child from being yelled at. I wanted him to parent like I did. It was not what the kids needed either – to see me going against their father. It was one of those periods I was talking about during the hard times. After, I would think – *kudos for not yelling at the kids, and next time let's try not to yell at Scott!* Progress Mama – not perfection. That right there was big progress. We are all doing the best we can at any given minute with the emotional capacity we have at the time. Yelling is a rarity at our house now. We use a stern voice to get some points across. If you and your child have a tendency at the moment to yell, you will begin to notice that as your yelling decreases so will your child's yelling.

Do my kids still yell? For sure. It is part of their unpacking and their level of maturity and the tools they have at the moment. 100%. Has it decreased dramatically? 100%! Try it out. Being able to pause and take a breath in between the stimulus and your response will change your life. Like the great Ghandi said: 'Be the change you want to see in the world.' I believe in you.

The power is in the pause.

Breathe.

My marriage to Scott means the world to me and looks nothing like it did 8 years ago. It has taken patience, an amount of patience I didn't think I had in me. As I share my stories at speaking events, workshops, with my coaching mums and dads and new friends, I thank the universe that I didn't walk out on my marriage to this remarkable man that horrible day. I am proud of the level of commitment, discipline and hard work we have put in to get to a place of acceptance and awareness of each other's differences, needs and wants. Discipline comes from the latin word 'discēre - to learn or to cut off. I was relearning how to be his wife while cutting off the stories of the past. The version of love that we were running needed a complete revival to get us to where we are now.

I get to fall in love with him again every day. I get to watch him be a father that is perfect, whole and complete for his children. I have watched him stand in all his vulnerabilities and kick what society says a father should do to the kerb and be the father his kids need him to be. Be the father that his heart knows he was put here on earth to be. He is a father that his father would be so proud of. Be a father that Billy can model from. He kisses and cuddles those kids to the point where they beg him to stop. He tells them how proud of them he is. He helps them feel good about themselves, and helps them understand their differences and that they are human, and reassures them that there is nothing wrong with them when they question that. He tells me what a wonderful job I am doing and that our kids are lucky I am their mother. He tells me how proud of me he is, and how thankful he is for me leading the charge – doing all the research – reading the books – going first – taking the kids to 90% of the appointments.

He is our safe place to fall.

He is our rock.

He is the hardest worker we know.

He has our backs.

He is ours, and we love him more than all the peanut butter Reece's chocolates in the galaxies (they are his favourite!).

Chapter 6...

WHAT WE DID.

I wanted to run through what we did here at the Martin house on our journey and what we do now (at the time of writing this book with the disclaimer that our family is on an open and curious journey). I was thinking this morning that in the lead up to diagnosis I kept reading, 'between the age of 5 and 9 are the hardest'. It seemed that everywhere I turned I was hit smack-bang in the face with this. Billy was just over 5 at the time when I kept stumbling across it, and I would think to myself, 'I'm not gonna make it. Billy isn't going to make it. Our family isn't going to make it through the next 4 years!' Billy just turned 10, and when this book is in my hands Zhema will be 9. I can say we have made it. I can also understand why I kept reading it was a hard time. I don't generally agree it will be the hardest, as I don't know what is to come, but I do agree it is hard. Hard because they are so little and as parents we were so scared and scattered and confused. Not a great start.

For us, we can see as they have grown older, the awareness and knowledge they have increased. They can understand their gifts, challenges and wiring more and more. It is also a time where, as a mother, my knowledge starts from zero and builds daily. As I educate myself, I can educate my children more. It makes complete sense now.

Let's all stop and take a big deep breath. In through your nose, down through your heart, into your belly and a long slow exhale out through your mouth. And again. You are going to make it. You are more than going to make it – you are going to make it and see that Autism is like a rocket ship ride to your own evolution. You are going to see and feel the world through a unique lens. You are going to be given an opportunity for you to be a lotus and rise out of the mud. Every day. You are the lotus. Every night you close up, put yourself to rest and rejuvenate, then each morning you rise again, up from the mud and open to your beautiful, unique self.

I often look into the kids' eyes and reflect back to when Billy was 4 and Zhema was 3 and I started down the road of getting help and support. What followed was a mother desperate for help. When you are in a desperate state of mind, I don't believe we make our best decisions. I was coming from a place of lack. More so, I couldn't quieten my mind enough to see what was really working in those early days and what wasn't. Nor was I settled and present enough: I ended up buying this, that and the other, and didn't set aside the time that was required to get the most benefit out of the product/tool or to see if it even had a benefit.

As I say, we are all doing the best we can at the time with the emotional capacity we have.

Fact.

I have been into natural therapies since I was 17. I have never felt so grateful for Western medicine than I do today. I believe natural therapies can be the answer to a lot of things in life, and if not the answer a wonderful support system, and now I know Western medicine certainly has a place in my family's life for now.

The kids saw a homeopath in the early years. They also had some chiropractic treatments and naturopathy. They all bring something different to the table for me. They both saw OT's. When Billy was in prep I started to buy anything that was suggested. I was grasping. The noise in my head was getting louder and louder and I was starting to get a bit manic. We had the spikey sitting wedge for him to sit on at the dinner table. We had the brush to brush his body every morning and night. I bought the electric toothbrushes as that puts 'data' into their bodies like the brush. We trialled the weighted blanket and they didn't like it. Then they loved it. Now they hate it.

I bought what seemed like every sensory toy, fidget cube, pencil clasp, slope boards, wobble stools, swings… that I could find on the sensory sites. I would sit the kids down and ask them to pick what they wanted. Did they use them at school or home? Some of them. Did I keep buying them in desperation? Yes. I thought 'this one' would be 'the one'. One thing they did use a fair bit was the therapy putty to help strengthen their hand and finger muscles (and Zhema snuck hers into bed one night, fell asleep and yep – we ended up having to throw out her PJs, and the sheet and doona cover are now on hand for rags!). They have a crash mat, and it is sooooo good. They have a vibration cushion which they sit and lay on and cuddle. Pressure vests. What I want to point out here is in the early days I bought everything and anything. What I would do differently is not buy as much and give things more time. I know, for me, having too many choices can be overwhelming. I was overwhelmed.

They were both put through a neonatal reflexes program over a few months. Billy was identified as having a tongue and lip tie, and we had that lasered and he had the ongoing treatment after that to ensure the release remained. It still blows me away how far he can stretch his tongue now. If I showed you the picture of the hole that was under his tongue from the release, your stomach would be in your throat. I don't have any regrets getting it done. I bought some really cool books.

We invested our hearts and had everything crossed while using natural supplements and vitamin support. I had to flog that natural medicine path until I knew in my gut that I had done all I could within my capabilities before I would even take on the concept of Western medicine.

Western medicine doesn't work for everyone. It is such a personal decision and I am not going to debate any of the pros and cons. To be honest, I stopped Googling the medication. My choice. Scott and I put our trust in our paediatrician and let go. Our choice. We have had to have a few changes along the way, and that is heart wrenching. You wouldn't wish it on your child. You are changing because they are going backwards and then the weaning happens and it can be rocky. My kids will always be Autistic, and maybe one day they won't be on medication. Either way, I believe in my heart the support of medication has been a game changer.

Their progress is something that years ago I didn't think was possible with my limited knowledge and limiting beliefs. I'm holding back tears now. These kids do the hard work. 24/7. Therapy isn't always easy, although their therapists try and make it as fun as they can. There have been times they didn't want to go, and we would talk to them about the 'why' and they would always go. 2 inspiring, hard-working kids. I couldn't be more proud of the 2 champions I get to call my children. I tell them every day that they are everything I ever dreamed of having in a son and daughter. They love hearing that.

These kids are so young to be going through this. The more care you give yourself, the more you can show up for them. The more you nourish yourself, the more you can nourish your children.

One of the best things we have done is put the mini trampoline in our lounge room. It is gold. Mum gave it to us. So grateful. The kids jump on the tramp during dinner, they jump on it at random times. We have a little course they do that we got from our OT: they do 4 big squat jumps on the floor, jump up on the tramp, 5 jumps on the tramp, jump up onto the lounge, jump along the lounge then do a big jump and crash their body onto the crash mat. It does wonders for the proprioception and regulation.

Once you throw out the rule book on parenting and how your kids 'should be', your life will relax a little. You will relax a little. A lot, actually. Zhema watches the TV upside down. She wiggles and moves. Some days they eat their dinner standing. Some days laying down watching TV. They wander away not even knowing they have, and you keep asking them back to the table time and time again. Other times they can sit down and eat their dinner. You can't pick it. We recently had a high tea at my mum's place for my niece's birthday, and I looked over at Scott and said, 'Look at the kids,' and I smiled. Everyone was sitting at the table enjoying the most amazing high tea I have ever seen put on by my mother, and our 2 kids bottoms didn't hit their chairs. It is just how it is at this present time. Always changing. As parents, we could have been in argument with that and constantly fought with them to sit down or we could just smile and let them move their bodies and walk around and enjoy the precious time with our extended family. Which one sounds better to you? My family doesn't even notice it anymore. I still notice, and my heart smiles.

To diagnose or not?

This is such a personal thing, and from our side, diagnosis was a great decision. I know so many mothers now that have said to me, 'I know our child shows signs of this, that or the other,' or 'I know my child is on the spectrum,' and they choose not to go down the diagnosis journey. That is the beauty of life – we all have choices and they are ours to own. Diagnosis for our kids was right for us. Looking back, Billy was going downhill fast, and we were all going down with him. Scott and I were confused. We couldn't work it out. We couldn't work out how to help him or help ourselves. Getting the right diagnosis for Billy, Zhema and Scott was like being in a dark, dark cave for years, scared out of our minds, fearing we would be stuck here for the rest of our lives, then suddenly you hear a noise and you know it is help. You know in your cells that things are going to get better. You don't quite know how it will all work out in that exact moment, but you know it's going to get better than it is right now.

I have always said that knowledge has been power to me on this Autism journey. Without the diagnosis, I wouldn't have the knowledge I do today. I wouldn't have the acceptance of the wiring that my family runs. I don't think I would have gotten to the level of radical love that I have for myself and my family. For humanity. A love I didn't even know existed. I wouldn't have the level of understanding and acceptance for the way they deal with their difficulties and challenges. The diagnosis has given me an opening in my heart for me to hold space for my family. Space for them to be themselves. Space for them to learn and at times learn the hard way. I literally can't imagine what our life would be like if we kept battling on and thinking they would snap out of it. They would grow up. They would eventually respond to discipline. I don't have to imagine and if I did, I would be wasting my precious time.

Diagnosis gave Scott and I even more understanding around the wiring and the troubles they were experiencing, and helped us in making the decisions we have. My face is smiling, and I can feel my heart expand right now as I type this. I remember looking at Billy one day while he was on the lounge watching TV and thinking that he will have a good life. A really good life. A great life! I hadn't felt that in years. Not since he was a little toddler.

When your child is struggling day in and day out and nothing you seem to do has any significant impact on their life, you start fearing the worst. Terrible thoughts about them not having any friends, being alone at lunch time, not being invited to playdates and parties, not growing up with a village of mates that have their back, not having the emotional ability to form deep relationships, not being able to experience that beautiful life full of love and laughs. I'm not saying that they must experience life 'like this' to be truly happy – I am saying that I was full of fear that they wouldn't be able to experience the life that they wanted. Big difference. For Billy, back then, he wanted to play with kids and when he did after a certain time it would get too much and things would go south, and he would end up distressed or in trouble. The feedback he was constantly getting was that most of what he did was wrong. Once things had calmed, he was totally aware of his part in it all and would be so upset. His brain would fire firefirefirefire, and he would react reactreactreact. It broke his heart.

When your child is aware of their differences and wants to change them and can't – that breaks your heart. Holding space in those moments takes courage as a parent. Holding space so they don't feel like they have a disorder is courage in motion.

One thing about diagnosis that I am still struggling with is the term Disorder in the ASD label. That I can say is the negative for me about diagnosis. I have had a few conversations with a new friend I have who is Autistic around how to refer to my kids and Autism in general, and it is really interesting. I have found that when I say 'high functioning', people pretty much think 'they are fine'. The term 'Asperger's' is on the way out. There was a time that I refused to say Autism Spectrum Disorder because of the term disorder. Autistic as first person language is what feels aligned for me.

WRAPPING IT UP

In June 2018, after 25 years of a fulfilling and successful career in finance and banking, I walked away. It was 1 year before that my son, husband and daughter were diagnosed with Autism. In June 2017, my life changed forever. For the better.

One by one, and in that order, the diagnoses were handed over. What followed in that next 365 days for me was the universe unravelling its bigger plans. In that 12 months I was stripped bare. Naked. I got the chance to go deep within. To get out of my head and into my heart. To lay in the dark and rumble with the pain until I could see the light and the lesson. I got to sift through my morals and values and see what I wanted to keep with me. The rest I left behind. I got to look at who was in my village and why they were there. I face planted as I unpacked 42 years of life. I face planted a lot. I stood and faced fears front on and I ran from some of them until they chewed me up and spat me out enough times to stop and do what needed to be done. I sat with feelings that I hope other mothers don't have to. I've felt the pain of my husband as he travelled his own path of vulnerabilities and watched on in awe as he gets to know himself with Autism wiring at 48.

What happened internally in that 12 months has changed my destiny. It has opened me to a life of service. A life of advocacy. Every day I have either spoken and engaged with a mother of a child on the spectrum, someone about life on the spectrum, read an article, completed part or all of a course, watched a webinar or held space for someone touched by Autism. Every. Day. Not a day has gone by since diagnosis where I have not been present in some way in this new space.

It is in every breath I take.

Every day there was a voice about helping the mother in the dark. Helping the mother who is on a similar path. Helping a mother see her best self. Helping a mother unpack so she can see the answers that she holds within. Helping a mother by holding a confidential and safe space where she can share her dark times, her feelings, her wins. A space where she will move through the chaos and confusion and into calm and clarity. A space where I can invite her to use tools and practices for herself, not just her children. I answered that voice and ate another surrender sandwich and moved into coaching mothers who are parenting kids on the spectrum. Speaking at conferences and workshops. I got out of my head and into my heart. Many times a day. I answered the voice to write this book, knowing it is one of a few books I have in me. Knowing it won't be perfect. Knowing there is so much of our story that I can't put in writing and I will never know until the kids are older if I have crossed the line with them in what I have written.

I answered these callings to honour my soul and honour you, the mother, the father.

And so began another chapter in my life. For 25 years, I knew what I was doing in my 'work'. For 25 years, I had nailed it 5 days a week. I then entered the land of not knowing. The land of building a community. Building the know, like and trust factor that every marketing person will speak to you about. Building something from the ground up. It wasn't just building a house using someone else's products: it was coming out into the world with my story and my family's story. It was putting myself on the line. And I did. Did I imagine it would be so hard and rewarding? No. I did think it was going to be pretty easy and all happen pretty quickly? Wrong. I have had what one may refer to as a colourful life.I have rebounded back more times than I could count.I am resilient and a bounce back master.I didn't think about having to use different technologies and systems.I get easily frustrated with technology and I didn't calculate the emotional and physical toll it would all take.

I walked away and did my coaching certification and coached under a mentor and started writing my book. I used to conduct a meditation and relaxation class which brought so much inner peace, calm and clarity to those who attended. I smashed out 80% of the book in around 8 weeks, I think. Boom. I was like a steam train. One track. One focus and smashed it. Then, it stopped. All of sudden I wouldn't go near this book. It was like it didn't exist.

Everyone kept asking how it was going, and I would say, 'Good, and I'm going to start back on it on Monday.' Good old Monday. We can put so much pressure on that day. Monday never came. What did come was a few months of saying to myself, 'Scott doesn't accept himself as Autistic. I can't publish this book when he only sees himself as having traits and not fully Autistic. I can't keep hosting speaking events and workshops and saying my family is on the spectrum and running Autisticwiringuntil he does accept it.' I ran this story day in day out. I had another one of those hard conversations and spoke to Scott. He did see himself as only having traits. We discussed everything, and we were clear. He is Autistic. Another surrender sandwich for Scott to chow down.

That man is so damn brave and courageous.

Nothing happened with the book. It was now 17 months since my family was diagnosed and nearly 5 months since I started writing the book. Why was I not finishing my book? Because I was writing the book and going around saying I was a neurotypical mother with a family on the spectrum. At this point, I had done 17 months of educating myself. I had a special interest in females and Autism because Zhema's struggles are different to Billy's, and they can be harder as a parent to navigate. All that kept coming up was that the statistics of girls being undiagnosed were huge. The testing was set up for boys and males. The more I stepped into this area of females, the louder the voice became. I wasn't the neurotypical mother. I was the Autistic mother. I began reflecting on my life since I was 5 and putting all the pieces together. Bit by bit, piece by piece, it was all there in front of me.

The struggle to understand girls, their facial expressions and what they were interested in. The anxiety around what I was going to wear every day. The resistance around showering and I still have the resistance today and often skip showering. Numbing my 'big feelings' with alcohol and recreational drugs from my late teens to late 20's. Talking too much in class. Distracting others and being easily distracted. Eating disorders. So many things make perfect sense now. So grateful to know me more now than I ever have. Never have I been so content to be me.

I had become friends with an amazing woman, Kirsty Forbes, who is from InTune Pathways and is Autistic/ADHD-er/PDA-er. I asked her some questions and she answered them. This woman is intelligent, connected and honest. That day was a day I will never forget. What followed was a 2-week period where all my life flashed in front of me. All the trauma and pain and confusion of the last 38 years from when I was 5 surfaced. It is interesting in reflecting that all the great things I have achieved from my Autism didn't come to mind during those 2 weeks. I had a lot of support from 2 great friends during those 2 weeks. I knew what the next step was and I took it.

1 week before my 43rd birthday, I was given the gift of being diagnosed with Autism. It was the best birthday present I have ever been given. As I put the finishing touches on this book, I have had my diagnosis for just over a year. For a year , I have known that nothing is wrong with me. That missing pill I have been chasing for 38 years isn't needed.

Nothing is missing.

And here I am, finishing my book.

Here I am as Zoe Martin.

It has been a crazy few months. First thing was to tell my family, and they are just the best. So much love and acceptance for me. They have loved me through all of this, and at times, in my teens and 20s, that would have been a little difficult. Then it was to tell my close friends. It started to get super draining, the thought of it all, so I did the Facebook post, and what a relief. It's out. It is done. I have had so many comments from people. It has been such an eye opening experience.

You don't look Autistic.

You look Autistic.

I knew in your FB lives that you were Asperger's.

What level are you?

How can they fix that?

I'm sorry to hear that.

I was telling a friend the other day that these are things that people say to our children or say to us as parents about our children, and it was awesome for me to go first and be on the receiving end of these. No harm or malice was meant by anyone in what they said to me. At all. They were legit friends.

Oh bless. I find it really interesting, and I am so grateful to experience this first hand. So grateful. At 43, I get to sit with it, process it and be of service to Autism and to the greater good.

Clearly, I am in the early days of processing all of this and getting to know my Autism deeply. I am so excited for the next chapter of my life. I am so excited to get to know myself as an Autistic woman. It's so reassuring as I get to unpack and acknowledge what I do well in life which is: connection, love, holding space along with a million other things and then look at what I struggle with which is: executive functioning, showering, public places ... I now get to look into what supports my brain: health and my body. So I can operate at my best. I get to unleash a new level of compassion, gentleness and radical love on myself, which ripple out to my husband, children and humanity.

I smile at the benefit to myself, now I know. When you don't know, you don't know. I now know. I smile at the benefit that my work will be to mothers and children now that I know I am coming from an Autistic space. Limitless.

I am home. I am finally home. From the darkness comes my light. I am free to be me.

I am Zoe Martin.

Here is a letter I wrote 4 days after my diagnosis on 17/11/2018:

Hi Zoe,

Breathe.

When you don't know, you don't know. Now you know. Thank you for being brave.

Courage is another word that comes to mind. Thank you for listening to your inner voice. For honouring your intuition. For seeking answers to questions that you have been asking for 38 years.

As you travel the path of reflection, introspection and contemplation… go gently, my girl. Go softly. As you travel backwards and forwards… don't miss the now.

Through the gifts of my children, I find you. All of you. Through the safety of my husband, I contract and expand.

As you start to share your Autism with your family, friends and the world, your why will change. Flow, my girl, flow. The days of trying to be someone else are over. The world needs Zoe. Zoe Martin. Coach. Speaker. Author. Human.

I know you've known you were unique – extra unique, to be honest.

Now the world gets to know.

I love you. The Autistic you.

You have been a second-rate neurotypical girl.

Now shine as a first-rate Autistic woman.

Love, Zoe. Xxx

As I continue to ground down in who I am and who I am not, I get more and more clear in my message. I continue to expand into a greater consciousness. I don't have the finer details of my why all sorted out. I know I am here to serve. I know I am here and guided by my core values of hope, faith, purpose and love . I know that coaching and mentoring mothers and fathers who are leading neurodivergent children is my 'life's great work'. I know I love speaking at conferences, and at any event where people gather to empower, share and educate each other. I love to write, and there are more books in me. My personal story, the story of Making Peace with Me, will be next.

I know I will continue to face-plant and get back up. I know I will continue to honour my time in the dark as that is where my greatest growth is. I will continue to dance in the light and keep opening my heart to the beauty that lies within and in those around me. I will continue to be the best mother, wife, daughter, daughter in law, sister, aunty, cousin, sister in law, friend and human I can be. I will be transparent. I will show up. I will continue to remind myself that I am here, on earth, at this time, to be me. As for the rest, I lean into the uncertainty, the joy, the pain and I live in the question. I am supported by the universe, mother nature and my mentors. Life is here for the taking. I am going to take it.

Chapter 7...

TEAM MARTIN NOW.

We have a family motto that Scott came up with: 'Just love me.' We have many times of laughing, of cracking jokes, of family fun. We have times that are a big mess – sometimes with warning and sometimes without. We are learning to be compassionately flexible. We are learning our own family code. We discuss openly our gifts and how our wiring comes with a bag of super powers and a bag of super struggles. We talk about our darkness and our light. We remind ourselves we are human and that we are a neurodivergent family.

Scott and I are taking a lot of big breaths and circling back. We are doing the work, both within and with each other.

Our life is our life to create. We are all here on our own journeys united by blood and choice. Scott and I are learning a new language in our marriage. That is taking energy and commitment and time. Our love for each other is stronger than ever. My love for Scott continues to deepen and change as my love for myself continues to deepen and change. We are 100% committed to the happiness of each other and our family unit.

Little did we know 20 plus years ago that our path would lead us here. Having kids with neurodiversity puts a huge strain on a relationship and also has the power to strengthen beyond limits. We know first-hand why. Having 2 people in a relationship with neurodiversity puts a huge strain on a relationship.

Scott leads from the front with his commitment and loyalty. He does this in all areas of his life. He protects us, provides for us and fixes all he can. Traits that are extremely important to him. Our relationship will continue to head north towards the sun, moon and the stars. If we have made it this far, we will make it to the end. It will be filled with eating infinite surrender sandwiches and give and take. Daily doses of vulnerability, courage and bravery will continue. Forgiveness gets a run every day.

I am super excited to see where we are in another 10 years! Scott keeps saying that as long as he can play golf, I am wife of the year. He doesn't want to see my list for him to be husband of the year – hahahaha! Mine is a little longer -a walk outside in Mother Nature, yoga and green juice…….

The kids are thriving in their own unique way in this life. They are facing a lot of tough times and their resilience is growing. They will have many testing times as Autistic humans and they are going to have Scott and I in their corner cheering them on the whole way. They are overcoming fears and their confidence in growing. They are so young and have so much yet to navigate.

They are putting their hands up to try new things, knowing they have a safety net of love to catch them if they fall. Their ability to articulate their emotions and feelings continues to amaze me as they mature. They are cultivating an awareness of the impact they have in this world. I am helping them with the realisation that their words create their life. They are face planting and dusting themselves off. They are certainly experiencing the full range of the human emotions a little earlier than most. I feel that is part of our wiring.

I witness their hearts opening to new levels as my heart explodes to new levels! We have just had the best xmas, new year and family vacation we have ever had. So much connection. Not one meltdown. Scott and I being present. There is no way this would have been achieved without Scott and I committing to being fully present and meeting all 4 of us where we are at. We worked as a team and were skilled to read our children, read the signs and implement the strategies that work for us. We are getting comments almost daily on how far the kids have come. How far our family has come. This is the accumulation of so many things. I couldn't be prouder of my family and myself and I am also grounded in the reality of this not always being the case yet I celebrate the wins!!!

This life is full of change, and emotional balance is important. Kindness is up the top of the list of what we want to instil in our kids. Helping them with change is key in a world where things are changing at a rapid pace. Helping them create space in their minds to just 'be' in a world where our sensors are being overloaded. Teaching them mind and body connection and being able to read their internal engines. Teaching them that taking a break is self care, to take time out for their brains and hearts is needed. Educating them on Autism wiring is on ongoing task. They have also been diagnosed with ADHD/ADD and PDA. We hope as parents we are equipping them with a strong sense of self. A strong sense of family and tribe. A strong sense that despite our official diagnosis containing the word 'disorder', that we are whole and complete and not out of order.

We are very much in order.

As each moment passes, I am constantly reminded that they are not mine to own. They are a gift I have been given and their lives are theirs to live. I am honoured to be their sherpa for a short time. I feel like a Sherpa leading them up Mt Everest. Leading the way, yet it is them who will take the steps. I can't take the steps for them.

Taking back my identity and healing my past has let me give my children and husband back their identities. This truly has changed my life. I am responsible for my actions and lack of action. That is it.

Zhema is a shining light. She radiates from a heart that will help change this world. She does Soul Scanning on me and Crystal Balancing. Phenomenal. This has all come from within her. Her inner knowing of the benefits of meditation and yoga is astounding. She is destined for greatness, just like her brother. She has just written her own Code of Honour. One of the codes is 'I commit to taking breaths when spiritual moments are hard.' This girl is a gift to this earth. She talks a lot about helping other kids with autism and adhd, especially kids with anxiety. I am so excited to see where her soul takes her. I will be cheering her on all the way. Since her ADHD/ADD diagnosis and help we have received with that, she is kicking goals academically. Really big goals. She is mastering her emotions bit by bit and can forgive within seconds. She is growing into an exceptional young girl. A girl I am so proud to call my daughter. A girl that teaches me something new every day. Every. Day.

Billy has started at a new school and we couldn't be prouder of him. Such huge changes. Huge. Each day he does his best. He is fiercely competitive. Billy is so fun to be around. I love his passion for making money and the way he can map out ideas and make bring them into fruition. His mind continues to astonish me and having him in my life has been the best. He keeps my integrity in check and his memory is so helpful to his mum who seems to forget…many things! The kid is a champion and being his mother is a privilege I don't take lightly.

Our wonderful homeopath said the day she met him when he was 3 that he would be famous. She could see his name – 'Billy Martin' – up in lights. I agree. He has a business mind and had an extremely successful lemonade stand while we were camping one year. He is a driven boy with so much to offer in this life. His brain never stops and he is always dreaming something up and will one day pay cash for a Lamborghini.

He has the kindest heart, the best smile and is smart, funny and very handsome!

Being human, we don't know what the future will hold. We get to turn up each day and create our life and the universe does the rest. My kids have a brilliant future ahead. They have the unconditional love and support of their parents. Always and in all-ways. They have a family and village that loves them today, just as they are. Scott and I are privileged to have that love and support, too.

As I rise each day with gratitude and embrace our diversity as a family, we will continue through this human experience, facing the full range of emotions with our Autistic/ADHD/ADD/PDA wiring. I know the answers are within honouring our feelings, all of them. It is hard and it is freeing. I lead by honouring my light and my dark. We honour our mess and we honour our greatness.

There are no limits on what is possible for Team Martin.

When I reflect on where we started 6 years ago when Billy was 4 and our hero's journey really began, I can literally feel my heart in my chest. At times I burst into tears with gratitude. I have cried so many times while writing this book. It has been a wonderful experience for me. At times I want to yell 'I did it! We did it!' We were a family living in fear with little moments of good times. Now, we are family living in love with little moments of fear. My mum always says we are either living from fear or love, and now, our predominate state is love.

I love my family, my life, and my autistic/ADHD/PDA-er self.

I love you too.

what next

Zoe is in her genius coaching and mentoring parents across the world who have been gifted with autistic and neurodivergent children. She offers private coaching and the Sovereign Parents Circle for parents to gather in a group where the magic of connecting, healing and exploring new paradigms is so much easier with others that get it.

Zoe brings her heart, courage and extraordinary life experiences together with a toolkit like no other. Her mission is to help mothers and fathers return to love as soon as they can. To bring forth trust. Trust that they hold the answers. Trust they know their child better than anyone else. Trust in each other.

Your children, the way you parent, the way your family does this and doesn't do that - needs to make sense to no one - but your family. When you clear away the trauma, heal the past, make peace with the present, you now have space to intentionally build the life you are so worthy of living. Your brilliant future awaits.

Within the circle of her work, she gets to call upon an extensive range of modalities grounded in both science and energetic frequency (the seen and unseen). Her love of learning sees her hold certifications in coaching (Optimize Coach), epigenetics (ph360 Health Coach & ph360 Parenting Facilitator), communication (Parent Talk System - PTS), fitness (certificate 3 & 4 personal trainer), creating brilliant futures (Futurist) and meditation teacher.

She is currently Australia's only Transcendental Rebirth facilitator. She has a relentless love of learning and collaborating with her neurokin to bring to the surface tools that can help not only her own family but other neurodivergent families. Zoe runs retreats and loves to speak at conferences, workshops and in webinars.

There are more soul fuelled offerings underway and as for what the brilliant future holds…this is the great news….we get to create it…and Zoe is certainly doing that.

You can connect with Zoe by visiting zoemartin.com

Thank you:

I know I don't read this part in every book yet now I am writing my first book I know how important it is to the Author and I vow to not skip this again.

My husband Scott, thank you for giving me a second chance at love and life. There is no one else in this world I want to do life with but you. I love you. All of you. Thank you for deciphering the parts of this world I find confusing and for keeping our family safe.

Billy and Zhema, my love for you is sacred. Thank you for choosing me to be your mum. It is my greatest honour in this life on earth. I love you, every day.

Dad, its been 28yrs since I have hugged you yet I feel you with me more than ever and I know how proud of me you are. I am proud of you too. I love you.

Mum, I wouldn't be here if it wasn't for you. 15,996 days you have loved me and been there for me. You are more than I ever imagined in a mother. I love, respect and admire you. Thank you for showing me what unconditional loves looks and feels like.

Danny, thank you for being the greatest step dad and grandfather. Thank you for always listening to me rattle on about this and that. You are the best! I love you.

To my brothers David and Heath, thanks for making up the rest of Team Simpson and for all the dead arms, farts cupped in my face and the never ending love you both gave me. Being your little sister is super cool and I thank for you for gifting me sister in laws and the best nieces and nephews on the planet.

To the rest of my family, thank you for loving me all these years. For holding space for me and now my family. I hold you all so dear in my heart. I love you.

To my friends, thank you. If you've been around for the long haul. The ride has been interesting. If you have just joined the ride, I thank you. At this age I get to choose who are my friends are consciously. I choose you. I love you and thank you for loving me.

Kristy Forbes, I love you! Crossing your path has been one of the greatest experiences in my entire life. I thank Autism for this! When I am with you, I am all me. Every cell in my body relaxes. My amygdala can switch off and take a break. The conversations are deep. They are real. They are heart expanding and contracting.

Every interaction with you gives me permission to expand, trust and love even more. Let's just say that I also think we extremely funny and we can pull a face or 3. Knowing you is a privilege and thank you for using your voice and showing me what speaking one's truth looks like.

To Emma Barbato, I met you when I was lost in life. Motherhood wasn't what I thought it was going to be. I was frustrated. I wasn't going to settle for what I was creating at that time. My answers were within but I didn't know how to get to them. You opened doors to my soul I didn't know existed. You mentored me at a crucial time in my life. That day you physically knocked me down was a day I knew I could rise from anything. Anything. I carry a piece of you where ever I go. Two pieces of wisdom from you that changed me deeply where when you told me I was standing with my 1 finger in the air a little too long and that I was safe to look at the world through Scott's eyes. Bless you woman! "The struggle begins when we lower our standards to soothe our fears". I love you.

To Susana Frioni, thank you for guiding me back to my intuition, holding space for me to open my heart again. To help me see my worthiness to access and play in my land of plenty.

To Katerina Satori, I honour you and your legacy here on earth. Your grace, love and light stays with me in every breath. I can hear us laughing and I can hear me crying. Divine timing at work and my life is forever richer for you being part of it. love you.

To Ivonne Delaflor, you were the first woman I met who has an Autistic child and spoke directly to my heart in a way I haven't experienced. You triggered parts of me that the world needs to see. You encouraged me and cheered me on to keep using my voice for the greater good – for Autism. You took the time to honour me exactly when I needed it...when I was swimming in fear. Travelling to America to complete the Transcendental Rebirthing Certification with you in August 2019 altered my perception of both myself and this world. The healing that took place and continues, allowed me to connect to my essence. Linages cleared of trauma. I honour you. Thank you for all you do in this world. I love you.

PB, here you are, in the thank you section of my book. The gentle tears of gratitude come from my heart and slide down my cheeks as I type this. It has been 14 months that you have been my 'Business Coach' and my entire world has changed from knowing and working with you. You lead me with integrity, grace and honesty that takes me to my edges...and beyond. You call it when it needs to be called. You cheer me on with a vibration of love. I've been scared and tried to run and every time, you have held my hand and guided me back, to my purpose. So much love and a billion high fives for you PB.

Maja, I am so grateful to PB for being the bridge that led me to you. Thank you for hearing me. Thank you all the times you challenged me when I wanted to make changes to the layout of this book. I was hiding behind fear and perfection and a whole bunch of other uncertainties and you can feel that and every time, helped me step forward. Your energy, creativity, passion and unwavering belief in bringing my story to the world now is why this book is here in 2020 and not 2030. From my soul to yours, thank you.

To Asaya, dreaming with you brings laughter, questioning and new depth to the edges of my life. So many memories in what is no time at all. The trajectory of my being has pivoted after every encounter. Doing life on earth with you is safe, fun and infinite. Thank you.

To Jess Nelson - my editor, thank you for answering my call out for help. My goodness. Talk about getting more than I dreamed of! You are honest. You are the real deal. Your heart is huge. You get it. You live it. Your suggestions were bang on every time. Thank you for saying yes to me. You are a gift to this world and you matter.

To my neighbours, 13 years ago we built this house not knowing who would build around us and when. I live in the best street ever. I will never forget the kindness you show us. To Paul writing 'It's a boy' on our fence when Billy was born and Lyn for all your encouragement (and donations to the kids). Kirstyn bringing over hot food to our little wedding party which is a whole other story and her continuous unconditional love for all that we are, and are not. To Brett and Christian for all the time you give to Billy. To Darren for allowing me and the toddlers to run a muck at his house on the week ends when I was clearing struggling with motherhood and Sandra for all the laughs and grounding moments. Sam and Lee for talking to my kids when they would be bouncing on the trampoline so high to ensure they could see you over the fence and all your support and smiles. To Kel, Gaz and the girls – gosh – thank you for the chats, the reassurance, the help, the acceptance. To the Lazlo's – I am so grateful for the positivity and joy you bring. To the Grady's – it is such a blessing to have the frequency of your family in our life.

To Tom Law, we have had many conversations over the last 6 years and one that I hold close is that day I was walking along the waterfront and you gave me a copy of your book. Your unwavering belief in me is something I treasure. You have continued to call me forward to finish this book. You are a man I respect and knowing you is a privilege.

To Deb my publisher, thank you for your patience and your help. I could feel it was hard for you to keep up with at times. Not hearing anything from me for months and months then you would get an email with changes along with asking the same questions again like 'how long is it from when I give you the manuscript to being able to have it in my hands?' Thank you for seeing it through with me.

To Alex, thank you for doing the initial edit. I remember being so anxious and questioning your process and kept waiting for you to come back and say that is all garbage and suggesting that I start again. Fear! You didn't. Thank you for being so patient with me, so kind with your words and helping me to see through my doubts.

To me, thank you for honouring your voice. Thank you for getting still so you could hear your soul. Thank you for pushing through the fears to experience freedom on the other side. Thank you for being brave in going for diagnosis. Thank you for taking off the masks and letting Zoe honour and speak her truth. With love, grace and gratitude, thank you.

WHERE TO FIND ZOE

www.zoemartin.com

FB @zoemartin.calm

Instagram @zoemartin.calm

www.ingramcontent.com/pod-product-compliance
Lightning Source LLC
Chambersburg PA
CBHW020321010526
44107CB00054B/1935